Contents

Introduction

by Sylvan Barnet

"Stand back to survey the whole." So runs an ancient bit of advice to the literary critic. Critics who follow this advice see in *The Merchant of Venice* the broad outline of a comedy (not merely a play with jests, but a play that ends happily) and they insist on interpreting the details according to this pattern. For them, the villain in the comedy must be entirely villainous, or, rather, comically villainous; he cannot for a moment gain the audience's sympathy. When they come, for example, to Shylock's "Hath not a Jew eyes?" they insist—because they are thinking of a pervasive comic plot—that the speech is comic and evokes no compassion. But there is another ancient bit of advice, urging the literary critic to "stand close so that you may be fully taken by the details." Critics of *The Merchant of Venice* who follow this advice often take Shylock to their hearts; they seize on a detail and dwell on it until it obscures the rest of the play, telling us, for example, how difficult life must have been for a Jewish widower in Venice. The trick is to combine the two approaches, to see the large pattern as helping us to interpret the details and also to see the details as helping to shape the pattern.

We can never see the play exactly as the Elizabethans saw it, of course, but we can make at least some effort to approach their vision. We can try, that is, to guard against grossly simplifying it because of our modern prejudices. If we can see the play, even in only a small degree, as they may have seen it, we may find it a richer thing than the play we see only with our twentieth-century eyes. The first thing we ought to try to do is to understand that although the word "Jew" echoes throughout the play, it is not in any important sense a play about Jews as we know them. Jews were banished from England in 1290, and the few that there were in Shakespeare's London practiced their faith secretly. The play is not an Ibsenite or Shavian treatise on "the Jewish problem"; for the Elizabethans there was no "Jewish problem," no mass of unassimilated Jews. True, Rodrigo Lopez, physician to Queen Elizabeth I and a member of the Church of England though of Jewish descent, evoked anti-Semitic remarks in 1594 when he was hanged, drawn, and quartered on a charge of treason, but the play is not about

1

that sad affair or about other Jews in London. What, then, is it about, if indeed it is "about" anything at all.

There are, of course, those who think that it is not about anything at all, that it is only a fairy tale, a delightful fantasy designed to enliven a couple of hours with elegant verbal music, and not to be taken seriously. Shakespeare himself sometimes seems to suggest (ironically?) that his comedies are not to be taken too seriously. *A Midsummer Night's Dream*, for example, ends with Puck suggesting that the audience may wish to think it has

> but slumb'red here
> While these visions did appear.
> And this weak and idle theme,
> No more yielding but a dream;

Twelfth Night ends with the suggestion that the world of the play is a brief, fragile, joyful construction that is surrounded by an enduring world of difficulties:

> A great while ago the world began,
> Hey, ho, the wind and the rain;
> But that's all one, our play is done,
> And we'll strive to please you every day.

Thus, in *The Living World of Shakespeare*, John Wain speaks of Shakespeare's "cockleshell boat of romantic comedy." Certainly, if one wants to see comedy as a frail boat, one can call attention to the fragility of such nonsense as a preposterous bond involving a pound of flesh, the simultaneous loss of all of a merchant's ships, their mysterious recovery, a father whose will requires his daughter to marry any man who chooses correctly among three caskets, and so on. These are clearly things from the world of fairy tale, and so too, in a way, is Shylock, a sort of male witch who craves the destruction of a Christian. (Almost the first thing that Shylock says about Antonio is, "I hate him for he is a Christian." He goes on to give an additional reason, that Antonio lessens Shylock's profits, but this second, more comprehensible reason does not displace the initial sheer malignancy of the sort associated with the villains of fairy tales.)

Let us assume, however, that the play *is* about something, and that it is not about the doings of Jews in England or in Venice. We can say, of course, that it is about a Jew who almost takes a pound of flesh from a Christian merchant, and it is about a young man who wins a young lady by passing a strange test. And we can go on to recognize the presence of Lorenzo and Jessica, the Gobbos, and others. But this is to summarize the plot, to say what happens rather than to say what the happenings add up to. When we turn from *what* happens to what the happenings are *about*—from plot to theme—we tend to allegorize, to see (perhaps) what we want to see. (But even when we are talking about plot, rather than theme, we may see what we want to. Critics who are partisans of Shylock, for example, often see the Christians as trivial and dishonest; specifically, they often claim that Portia hints to Bassanio, through a song that rhymes with "lead," that the leaden casket contains her portrait.) To say that the play adds up to something, that we make something out of it, and that it lends itself to a sort of allegorical interpretation is really not to say anything very daring about a work of literature. Surely literature is about something, and is not merely pretty sounds, though of course if at one end of the continuum of literature we have the realistic novel (which is "about" the real world), at the other end there are those songs in which sound almost completely triumphs over sense, such as "Double, double, toil and trouble; /Fire burn and cauldron bubble" in *Macbeth*. But even a realistic novel is a vision or interpretation of an aspect of life, something quite different from a newspaper that prints all of the random happenings that are thought to be of some interest to its readers. Art, that is, is symbolic, setting forth invented happenings that cohere into a pattern that somehow holds the interest of people in the real world. The dramatist tells a story that literally never happened, and in addition to setting forth the outside appearances of this story he gives it an inner meaning; we see the whole of it, as we do not see the whole of our own world. We understand not only how the people in this fictional world feel, but we form attitudes toward their feelings and their actions. We see (for example) a world of deluded people, or of people making the best of a bad lot, or of people living happy lives despite their own folly, or whatever. And the world on the stage, though evidently imagined (was there ever a father who married off his daughter in the fashion of Portia's father?), bears some sort of curious relation to our own world, even if the relation is no more than a vision of what we might wish our world to be or a vision of our idea of fun.

No brief statement about the theme of *The Merchant of Venice* (or of any other play) can adequately take account of every detail. Each detail modifies the stated theme, and finally we will end up saying, rightly, that the play's theme can only be stated by reading the play from the first line to the last. Still, we must often use shorthand approximations, and it seems reasonable to say, for a start, that *The Merchant of Venice* is largely about giving. The motto on the third casket, the one that contains Portia's picture, says "Who chooseth me must give and hazard all he hath." And if we look closely at the play, we can see that there is a great deal of talk about giving all. Bassanio has spent all he had; Antonio says that his funds "lie all unlocked" to Bassanio; Portia, when Bassanio has chosen her, says:

> Myself, and what is mine, to you and yours
> Is now converted. But now I was the lord
> Of this fair mansion, master of my servants,
> Queen o'er myself; and even now, but now,
> This house, these servants, and this same myself
> Are yours, my lord's. I give them with this ring.   (III.ii.166–71)

Lorenzo and Jessica give themselves to each other; Jessica gives some of Shylock's wealth to Lorenzo and lavishly exchanges ducats and jewels for trifles. Near the end of the play Antonio offers a second time to stake his life (in fact he says he will stake his soul) for Bassanio; and even the clown Launcelot decides (in Bassanio's words) "To leave a rich Jew's service to become / The follower of so poor a gentleman" as Bassanio. One risks or gives what one has, and, paradoxically, by such expenditure one flourishes the more. It is not only a question of giving money, of course; it is an attitude toward life. Bassanio has no money to give, but he can be generous nevertheless. When his friend Gratiano says to him, "I have a suit to you," Bassanio immediately replies, without first inquiring into the nature of the request, "You have obtained it." This motif of giving is most apparent in the business of wooing Portia, first because each suitor must pledge that if he fails he will not marry (that is, he must be willing to risk giving up the hope of re-creating himself in his children) and second, because Portia can be won only by a suitor who will "hazard all he hath"; in the play Bassanio is the only suitor who will act thus. Against these gestures of hazarding or venturing or risking, and of generous giving, stands Shylock, whose motto is

> Fast bind, fast find,
> A proverb never stale in thrifty mind.   (II.v.53–54)

This quotation conveniently brings us back to the question of why Shakespeare chose to make one of his central characters a Jew when there were, for all practical purposes, no Jews in England. Part of the answer, surely, is that in the popular mind the Jew stood for a way of life opposed to generosity. He stood for tight-fistedness, for usury, even though in England the usurers were Christians. It was commonly said of usurers, Francis Bacon recorded, that they "should have orange-tawny bonnets, because they do 'Judaize.'" If the idea was to create characters who are polar opposites, it would be dramatically fitting to set against Antonio—the generous Christian who is willing to risk his life for his friend, and who lends all freely—and against Bassanio, the generous Christian who hazards all—a usurious Jew, proud of his "well-won thrift," whose very first words in the play are "Three thousand ducats, well." Bassanio replies, "Ay, sir, for three months," to which Shylock replies, "For three months—well." The broad contrast, between lavish giving and cautious getting, is set forth in many ways, some of which have already been mentioned. And the outcome is that those who give, or who boldly risk the most—foolishly risk, from Shylock's point of view—are rewarded, while the cautious and calculating Shylock, seeking an opportunity to catch his opponent by framing an apparently foolproof bond, at last suffers great losses. Early in the play one of Antonio's friends needlessly cautions Antonio against too great a concern for "the world; / They lose it that do buy it with much care," unmistakably echoing Christ's words in Matthew 16:25–26: "For whosoever will save his life shall lose it. . . . For what is a man profited, if he shall gain the whole world, and lose his own soul?" It is not Antonio, however, but Shylock (and to a lesser degree Morocco and Aragon, judging from the caskets they choose) who manifests this sort of self-defeating care for the things of the world. It is Shylock who guards his money, who makes shrewd bargains, who insists on the fulfillment of the letter of the bond, and it is Shylock who is undone. A couplet that Portia speaks of Aragon is relevant to Shylock:

> O these deliberate [i.e., deliberative] fools. When they do choose,
> They have the wisdom by their wit to lose.   (II.ix.79–80)

(Aragon, scornful of "common spirits" as Shylock is scornful of the Venetians, chooses the casket that says, "Who chooseth me shall get as much as he deserves"; Shylock too looks forward to getting what he deserves: "What judgment shall I dread, doing no wrong?" and "My deeds upon my head! I crave the law.") For Shylock, the Christians are fools and prodigals, but in the play the prodigals triumph, finding that by giving and by risking they win love and happiness as well as money. (Though it might seem to us that Shylock too risks, or "hazards," he does not do so according to Elizabethan economic theory. His loan of 3000 ducats is assured, for Antonio is to forfeit a pound of flesh if Bassanio cannot repay the money on the date due. This means that Shylock, unlike a merchant-prince who risks his ships to the sea, or even a tradesman who cannot be certain that he will sell his goods at a profit, runs no risk at all, in contrast to the others, who will be less well-off if their ventures miscarry. Shylock cannot lose; he will either regain his principal or, even better, from his point of view, he will be able to kill Antonio.)

Speaking more generally, and moving a bit away from the play for a moment, the Renaissance Englishman knew the Jew only by reputation and by what he read in the Bible. There he would find Jesus saying to the Jews (in John 8:44): "Ye are of your father, the devil"; there (Matthew 27:25) he would find the Jews willingly acknowledging their complicity in the crucifixion: "His blood be on us, and on our chil-

dren"; there (Romans 1:29–32) he would find Paul denouncing the
Jews as "filled with all unrighteousness, wickedness, covetousness, mali-
ciousness, envy, murder, strife, deceit, malignity; whisperers, backbiters;
haters of God, insolent, haughty, boastful; inventors of evil things;
covenant-breakers; without natural affection, unmerciful." (This conception of the Jews as a people accursed by God because of their complicity in the Crucifixion has in some quarters survived to the present
day. In 1965 the Vatican Council found it necessary to declare that
"The Jews should not be presented as repudiated or cursed by God.")
As a man opposed to the values of love and life, the Jew of this tradition is the perfect symbol to counterpose to the generous, loving man.
In the play, not surprisingly, Shylock is often associated with the devil.
A few examples will have to suffice: when Shylock quotes from the
Bible, Antonio echoes Matthew 4:5 and Luke 4:10, saying "The devil
can cite Scripture for his purpose"; later Shylock's daughter will say
"Our house is hell"; and still later Portia will say that Shylock seeks to
engulf Antonio in "hellish cruelty." The broad opposition, then, is
between a hardhearted self-regarding diabolic figure and a group of
generous or (from a self-regarding point of view) prodigal people. Put
somewhat differently, it is a play about a man who often behaves
rather like a savage animal versus gentle and gentile people. Shylock
himself admits his fiercely passionate nature in several speeches, of
which two examples may be given:

> Thou call'dst me dog before thou hadst a cause,
> But since I am a dog, beware my fangs.   (III. iii. 6–7)

And, in the courtroom,

> So can I give no reason, nor I will not,
> More than a lodged hate and a certain loathing
> I bear Antonio.   (IV. i. 59–61)

And even the great speech "I am a Jew. Hath not a Jew eyes?" does not
reveal Shylock as a moral being, but rather stresses the physical or
animal identity of the Jew with all other men:

> If you prick us, do we not bleed? If you tickle us, do we not laugh? If you
> poison us, do we not die? And if you wrong us, shall we not revenge?
> If we are like you in the rest, we will resemble you in that. If a Jew
> wrong a Christian, what should his sufferance be by Christian example?
> Why revenge! The villainy you teach me I will execute, and it shall go
> hard but I will better the instruction.   (III. i. 61–69)

The speech is a brilliant piece of prose, revealing Shylock's psyche as
well as anything else in the play, but it certainly does not convince an
audience that there is no difference between men, or even between

the men in the play. A justification of revenge, it calls attention to a shared baseness; it does not recognize differences of the heart. It does not, for example, conceive of a mind like Antonio's, which later spares Shylock's life, and which harbors no resentment against Bassanio, though Antonio has fallen into Shylock's power because of Bassanio's prodigality. But of course more can be said on Shylock's behalf; nor is it merely our post-Dachau awareness that prevents us from regarding Shylock merely as a villain. As C. L. Barber points out in this book, Shakespeare occasionally lets us see Shylock not only as the gentiles see him, but as Shylock sees himself; to say this is not to say, however, that Shylock is right but only that we powerfully feel his claim.

The play is a comedy and, as Shakespeare's contemporary Thomas Heywood said in his *Apology for Actors* (1612), "comedies begin in trouble and end in peace." *The Merchant of Venice* begins with Antonio's melancholy and Bassanio's financial difficulties, and fairly soon gets Antonio into deeper trouble. It ends (after the playful quarrel about the rings) in peace, unless we brood upon Shylock's fate, in which case we find ourselves with those directors who, assuming that Shakespeare did not know when to stop, delete the entire fifth act, where Shylock does not appear. At least two things, however, must be said about Shylock's fate. First, the matter of forced conversion, which is surely distasteful to us, can probably never be palatable, even when we hear arguments to the effect that in Elizabethan eyes Antonio is doing Shylock a great favor by forcing him to become a Christian because Shylock's soul may thus be saved. The merits of forced conversion were much discussed in the past; suffice it to say that perhaps the Elizabethan audience saw in this episode of *The Merchant of Venice* a softening of Shylock's punishment, a gesture in the direction of bringing him into the community of civilized men, even if he must be brought in kicking and screaming. In fact, and this gets to the second point about Shylock's end, he does not kick and scream; when Portia turns the tables on him by insisting, as Shylock himself had insisted, on the letter of the bond, Shylock at first wheedles, and then collapses into "I am content." Here he sorely disappoints those who would see him as a tragic figure. As early as 1709 a kind of tragic Shylock was suggested, when Nicholas Rowe said:

> Though we have seen the play received and acted as a comedy, and the part of the Jew performed by an excellent comedian, yet I cannot but think that it was designed tragically by the author. There appears in it such a deadly spirit of revenge, such a savage fierceness and fellness, and such a bloody designation of cruelty and mischief, as cannot agree either with the style or character of comedy.

Notice, however, that Rowe, in suggesting that the part of Shylock was "designed tragically," is not suggesting that Shylock is, like the tragic heroes of Shakespeare's greatest tragedies, a man of noble character. Shakespeare's tragic heroes do indeed sometimes exhibit "fierceness and fellness," even "cruelty and mischief," but somehow they remain noble and heroic characters, characters willing to lay down their lives for some lofty ideal which they maintain even to the point of death. For Othello, it is of the utmost importance that Desdemona be as chaste as she looks; for Hamlet, it is of the utmost importance that the Danish court be freed from the corrupt Claudius. Othello, just before he kills himself, insists on telling his story to the world; Hamlet, dying, asks Horatio to tell his story for him, but what is Shylock's vision, and how does he affirm it? The man who had sworn to have a Christian's life, and who had declined thrice the money by saying, "An oath, an oath! I have an oath in heaven; / Shall I lay perjury on my soul?" does not nobly rise to reject the court's offer to spare his life if he will abandon his faith and convert to Christianity. Instead, he departs almost inarticulately, with "I am content," and "I am not well." These lines can of course be delivered with a dignity that contrasts favorably with Gratiano's jeers, but they can also be delivered with a whine that gives the lie to his earlier insistence on the holy claims of his oath. At the end, he betrays his oath, diminishes himself, and exposes himself to ridicule.

Attempts to elevate Shylock, it has already been mentioned, usually involve denigrating the Christians: Bassanio is a prodigal and a fortune hunter; Jessica (a convert to Christianity) is, in the words of Morris Carnovsky, who has acted the role of Shylock, "an apostate, really a little bitch, who willingly changes her religion to have a good time"; Lorenzo and Jessica steal; Portia lies (she tells Lorenzo that she will live in a monastery awaiting her husband's return, when in truth she goes to Venice to save his friend); Antonio mistreats Shylock, and so on. Some replies can be made. Bassanio is indubitably prodigal, but in the context of the play it can perhaps be argued that prodigality is linked to the virtue of generosity; and marriage where there is money is not in itself reprehensible, any more than is marriage where there is beauty. Bassanio indisputably loves Portia; of that there can be no doubt when one hears him speak in I.i.162–63 of the rich lady who "is fair and, fairer than that word, / Of wondrous virtues," or when one hears him in III.ii when he finds that he has chosen the correct casket and has thus won Portia. His probity is established not only by the testimony of his friends, and by Portia's love of him, but by the fact that he chooses correctly, for the choice clearly is a test of character rather than a matter of chance. Jessica's conversion—again, in the context of the play—is a conversion from a suffocating way of life ("Lock up my doors," Shylock instructs her) to a way of life that is not merely "a good time," to use Carnovsky's term, but one which recognizes that life flourishes most richly when it gives itself to another. Antonio's treatment of Shylock (he admits that he has spat upon Shylock) can probably never be made acceptable to us, but when we recall Shylock's own words, "I hate him for he is a Christian," we can perhaps grant to Antonio a complementary moral indignation. Antonio explains the contrast in their ways of life: "He seeks my life. His reason well I know: / I oft delivered from his forfeitures / Many that have at times made moan to me. / Therefore he hates me." This is not to say that in the world outside of the theater we approve of people who (like Bassanio) are rather free with other people's money or who (like Antonio) spit upon loan sharks (that is what Shylock is; he several times suggests his eagerness to "feed" upon the Christians); but in the festive world of this play it seems clear that the gentiles (and, by a pun, the gentles)[1] are conceived of as on the side of life, while the Jew is conceived of as on the side of a selfishness that constricts life. The gentiles, of course, are not faultless; Shylock calls attention, in IV.i.90ff., to the fact that their actions often fall short of what their Christian faith teaches them, and Gratiano shows Shylock no mercy in the trial scene. Still, it seems clear that there is a sharp distinction between Shylock's way of life on the one hand, and Portia's, Bassanio's, and Antonio's on the other. Not to recognize this is to open oneself to such an utterance as follows:

> Though he was rendered coldhearted by his vocation, made cruel by the insults that had been heaped upon him by everybody from the respectable Antonio to the very children in the streets, driven to desperation by his daughter, there is nothing to indicate that Shylock was congenitally coldhearted, cruel or desperate. On the contrary, it is clear that he had it in him, however deep down, to be humane, kindly, and patient, and his offer to Antonio of a loan without interest seems to have been a supreme effort of this submerged Shylock to come to the surface.[2]

When we return to the text, we see how far the critic has moved from the play. There is everything—in the play—to indicate that Shylock is "congenitally coldhearted, cruel, or desperate." He has a "Jewish heart," which is to say, again, in the context of the play, that he is wicked, an embodiment of a way of life that is spiritless. His first words upon seeing Antonio are an aside in which he confesses his "hate" for a Christian, and he goes on to say, "If I can catch him once upon the hip, / I will feed fat the ancient grudge I bear him. / . . . / Cursed

[1] Interestingly enough, Shakespeare himself was praised as "gentle," for example by Ben Jonson in a short poem "To the Reader," in the first collection of Shakespeare's plays, and again by Jonson in a longer poem in the same book, where Jonson speaks of Shakespeare's "gentle expressions." Judging from Shakespeare's own use of the word, a gentle person was one who by birth had virtues that manifested themselves in a potent mildness.

[2] Harold Goddard, *The Meaning of Shakespeare* (Chicago: University of Chicago Press, 1951), p. 100.

by my tribe / If I forgive him." Shortly thereafter he proposes the bond "in merry sport," but can it be doubted that he proposes it in the hope that it may afford him the chance to catch Antonio on the hip? Can one cogently argue that, in its context, his offer is indeed "humane, kindly, and patient"?

Possibly one can so argue; in the study of works of art the last word is never said. *The Merchant of Venice*, probably written about 1596, seems to have a family resemblance to such romantic comedies as *Much Ado About Nothing*, *As You Like It*, and *Twelfth Night*, all of which have handsome wooers, rich ladies, and spoilsports of one sort or another, and all of which end with the frustration of the spoilsports and the wedding of the amorous couples. We cannot, however, argue that this play *must* resemble the others, that Shylock *must* be seen as a spoilsport, although it seems to the editor of the present collection that the text of the play itself (and not merely a familiarity with Shakespeare's other comedies) makes the point quite clear. True, what the play means for readers and spectators today is quite as important as what we think it may have meant for readers and spectators 350 years ago, but nothing much is gained if for the Scylla of antiquarianism we substitute the Charybdis of contemporary impressionism that rejects the play because it presents an unfavorable picture of a Jew, or that seeks to rescue it by declaring, as Harry Golden does in *Only in America*, that it is a wholesale satire on hypocritical Christians. The essays that constitute this book seek to assist the reader in seeing the play for what it is, which is to say, in part, for what it means to thoughtful readers; but what the play is and means will very largely depend on what the reader makes out of it when he returns to it. He will then have to decide for himself the significance of such motifs as law and love, appearance and reality, seeing and sensing, getting and spending. Unless, of course, he remains convinced that the play is a "cockleshell boat" containing nothing.

The Merchants and the Jew of Venice:
Wealth's Communion and an Intruder

by C. L. Barber

Making Distinctions about the Use of Riches

The Merchant of Venice as a whole is not shaped by festivity in the relatively direct way that we have traced in *Love's Labour's Lost* and *A Midsummer Night's Dream*. The whirling away of daughter and ducats is just one episode in a complex plot which is based on story materials and worked out with much more concern for events, for what happens next, than there is in the two previous comedies. This play was probably written in 1596, at any rate fairly early in the first period of easy mastery which extends from *Romeo and Juliet*, *A Midsummer Night's Dream*, and *Richard II* through the Henry IV and V plays and *As You Like It* to *Julius Caesar* and *Twelfth Night*. At the opening of this period, the two comedies modeled directly on festivities represent a new departure, from which Shakespeare returns in *The Merchant of Venice* to write a comedy with a festive emphasis, but one which is rather more "a kind of history" and less "a gambold." The play's large structure is developed from traditions which are properly theatrical; it is not a theatrical adaptation of a social ritual. And yet analogies to social occasions and rituals prove to be useful in understanding the symbolic action. I shall be pursuing such analogies without suggesting, in most cases, that there is a direct influence from the social to the theatrical form. Shakespeare here is working with autonomous mastery, developing a style of comedy that makes a festive form for feeling and awareness out of all the theatrical elements, scene,

---

"The Merchants and the Jew of Venice: Wealth's Communion and an Intruder." From Shakespeare's Festive Comedy *by C. L. Barber (Princeton, N.J.: Princeton University Press, 1959), pp. 166–91. Copyright 1959 by the Princeton University Press. Reprinted, with the deletion of some footnotes, by permission of the publisher. Three pages comparing the festive mood of Nashe's* Summer's Last Will *and Testament with that of* The Merchant of Venice *are here omitted.*

speech, story, gesture, role which his astonishing art brought into organic combination.

Invocation and abuse, poetry and railing, romance and ridicule—we have seen repeatedly how such complementary gestures go to the festive celebration of life's powers, along with the complementary roles of revellers and kill-joys, wits and butts, insiders and intruders. What is mocked, what kind of intruder disturbs the revel and is baffled, depends on what particular sort of beneficence is being celebrated. *The Merchant of Venice*, as its title indicates, exhibits the beneficence of civilized wealth, the something-for-nothing which wealth gives to those who use it graciously to live together in a humanly knit group. It also deals, in the role of Shylock, with anxieties about money, and its power to set men at odds. Our econometric age makes us think of wealth chiefly as a practical matter, an abstract concern of work, not a tangible joy for festivity. But for the new commercial civilizations of the Renaissance, wealth glowed in luminous metal, shone in silks, perfumed the air in spices. Robert Wilson, already in the late eighties, wrote a pageant play in the manner of the moralities, *Three Lords and Three Ladies of London*, in which instead of Virtues, London's Pomp and London's Wealth walked gorgeously and smugly about the stage. Despite the terrible sufferings some sections of society were experiencing, the 1590's were a period when London was becoming conscious of itself as wealthy and cultivated, so that it could consider great commercial Venice as a prototype. And yet there were at the same time traditional suspicions of the profit motive and newly urgent anxieties about the power of money to disrupt human relations.[1] Robert Wilson also wrote, early in the eighties, a play called *The Three Ladies of London*, where instead of London's Wealth and Pomp we have Lady Lucar and the attitude towards her which her name implies. It was in expressing and so coping with these anxieties about money that Shakespeare developed in Shylock a comic antagonist far more important than any such figure had been in his earlier comedies. His play is still centered in the celebrants rather than the intruder, but Shylock's part is so fascinating that already in 1598 the comedy was entered in the stationer's register as "a book of the Merchant of Venice, or otherwise called the Jew of Venice." Shylock's name has become a byword because of the superb way that he embodies the evil side of the power of money, its ridiculous and pernicious consequences in anxiety and destructiveness. In creating him and setting him over against Antonio,

[1] A very useful background for understanding *Merch.* is provided by L. C. Knight's *Drama and Society in the Age of Jonson* (London, 1937) and by the fundamental social history which Mr. Knight used as one point of departure, R. H. Tawney's *Religion and the Rise of Capitalism* (New York, 1926).

Bassanio, Portia, and the rest, Shakespeare was making distinctions about the use of riches, not statistically, of course, but dynamically, as distinctions are made when a social group sorts people out, or when an organized social ritual does so. Shylock is the opposite of what the Venetians are; but at the same time he is an embodied irony, troublingly like them. So his role is like that of the scapegoat in many of the primitive rituals which Frazer has made familiar, a figure in whom the evils potential in a social organization are embodied, recognized and enjoyed during a period of license, and then in due course abused, ridiculed, and expelled.

The large role of the antagonist in *The Merchant of Venice* complicates the movement through release to clarification: instead of the single outgoing of *A Midsummer Night's Dream*, there are two phases. Initially there is a rapid, festive movement by which gay youth gets something for nothing, Lorenzo going masquing to win a Jessica gilded with ducats, and Bassanio sailing off like Jason to win the golden fleece in Belmont. But all this is done against a background of anxiety. We soon forget all about Egeus' threat in *A Midsummer Night's Dream*, but we are kept aware of Shylock's malice by a series of interposed scenes. Will Summer said wryly about the Harvest merrymakers in *Summer's Last Will and Testament*, "As lusty as they are, they run on the score with George's wife for their posset." We are made conscious that running on the score with Shylock is a very dangerous business, and no sooner is the joyous triumph accomplished at Belmont than Shylock's malice is set loose. It is only after the threat he poses has been met that the redemption of the prodigal can be completed by a return to Belmont.

The key question in evaluating the play is how this threat is met, whether the baffling of Shylock is meaningful or simply melodramatic. Certainly the plot, considered in outline, seems merely a prodigal's dream coming true: to have a rich friend who will set you up with one more loan so that you can marry a woman both beautiful and rich, girlishly yielding and masterful; and on top of that to get rid of the obligation of the loan because the old money bags from whom your friend got the money is proved to be so villainous that he does not deserve to be paid back! If one adds humanitarian and democratic indignation at anti-semitism, it is hard to see, from a distance, what there can be to say for the play: Shylock seems to be made a scapegoat in the crudest, most dishonest way. One can apologize for the plot, as Middleton Murry and Granville-Barker do, by observing that it is based on a fairy-story sort of tale, and that Shakespeare's method was not to change implausible story material, but to invent characters and motives which would make it acceptable and credible, moment by moment, on the stage. But it is inadequate to praise the play for delightful and poetic incoherence. Nor does it seem adequate to say, as E. E. Stoll does, that things just do go this way in comedy, where old rich men are always baffled by young and handsome lovers, lenders by borrowers. Stoll is certainly right, but the question is whether Shakespeare has done something more than merely appeal to the feelings any crowd has in a theater in favor of prodigal young lovers and against old misers. As I see it, he has expressed important things about the relations of love and hate to wealth. When he kept to old tales, he not only made plausible protagonists for them, but also, at any rate when his luck held, he brought up into a social focus deep symbolic meanings. Shylock is an ogre, as Middleton Murry said, but he is the ogre of money power. The old tale of the pound of flesh involved taking literally the proverbial metaphors about money-lenders "taking it out of the hide" of their victims, eating them up. Shakespeare keeps the unrealistic literal business, knife-sharpening and all; we accept it, because he makes it express real human attitudes:

> If I can catch him once upon the hip,
> I will feed fat the ancient grudge I bear him.[2]   (I.iii.47–48)

So too with the fairy-story caskets at Belmont: Shakespeare makes Bassanio's prodigal fortune meaningful as an expression of the triumph of human, social relations over the relations kept track of by accounting. The whole play dramatizes the conflict between triumph of human, social relations over the relations kept track of by accounting. The whole play dramatizes the conflict between the mechanisms of wealth and the masterful, social use of it. The happy ending, which abstractly considered as an event is hard to credit, and the treatment of Shylock, which abstractly considered as justice is hard to justify, *work* as we actually watch or read the play because these events express relief and triumph in the achievement of a distinction.

To see how this distinction is developed, we need to attend to the tangibles of imaginative design which are neglected in talking about plot. So, in the two first scenes, it is the seemingly incidental, random talk that establishes the gracious, opulent world of the Venetian gentlemen and of the "lady richly left" at Belmont, and so motivates Bassanio's later success. Wealth in this world is something profoundly

---

[2] It is striking that, along with the imagery of the money-lender feeding on his victims, there is the complementary prohibition Shylock mentions against eating with Christians; Shakespeare brings alive a primitive anxiety about feasting *with* people who might feast *on* you. And when Shylock violates his own taboo ("But yet I'll go in hate, to feed upon / The prodigal Christian." II.v.14–15) it is he who is caught upon the hip!

social, and it is relished without a trace of shame when Salerio and
Salanio open the play by telling Antonio how rich he is:

> Your mind is tossing on the ocean;
> There where your argosies with portly sail—
> Like signiors and rich burghers on the flood,
> Or, as it were, the pageants of the sea—
> Do overpeer the petty traffickers,
> That cursy to them, do them reverence,
> As they fly by them with their woven wings.   (I.i.8–14)

Professor Venezky points out that Elizabethan auditors would have
thought not only of the famous Venetian water ceremonies but also of
"colorfully decorated pageant barges" on the Thames or of "pageant
devices of huge ships which were drawn about in street shows." What is
crucial is the ceremonial, social feeling for wealth. Salerio and Salanio
do Antonio reverence just as the petty traffickers of the harbor salute his
ships, giving way to leave him "with better company" when Bassanio
and Gratiano arrive. He stands at ease, courteous, relaxed, melancholy
(but not about his fortunes, which are too large for worry), while
around him moves a shifting but close-knit group who "converse and
waste the time together" (III.iv.12), make merry, speak "an infinite deal
of nothing" (I.i.114), propose good times: "Good signiors, both, when
shall we laugh? say, when?" (I.i.66). When Bassanio is finally alone with
the royal merchant, he opens his mind with

> To you, Antonio,
> I owe the most, in money and in love.   (I.i.130–131)

Mark Van Doren, in his excellent chapter on this play, notes how these
lines summarize the gentleman's world where "there is no incompatibility between money and love. So too, one can add, in this community there is no conflict between enjoying Portia's beauty and her
wealth: "her sunny locks / Hang on her temples like a golden fleece."
When, a moment later, we see Portia mocking her suitors, the world
suggested is, again, one where standards are urbanely and humanly
social: the sad disposition of the county Palatine is rebuked because
(unlike Antonio's) it is "unmannerly." Yet already in the first scene,
though Shylock is not in question yet, the anxiety that dogs wealth is
suggested. In the lines which I have taken as an epigraph for this
chapter, Salerio's mind moves from attending church—from safety,
comfort and solidarity—through the playful association of the "holy
edifice of stone" with "dangerous rocks," to the thought that the so-
ciable luxuries of wealth are vulnerable to impersonal forces:

rocks,
Which, touching but my gentle vessel's side,
Would scatter all her spices on the stream,
Enrobe the roaring waters with my silks . . .   (I.i.31–34)

The destruction of what is cherished, of the civic and personal, by
ruthless impersonal forces is sensuously immediate in the wild waste
of shining silk on turbulent water, one of the magic, summary lines of
the play. Earlier there is a tender, solicitous suggestion that the vessel
is the more vulnerable because it is "gentle"—as later Antonio is gentle
and vulnerable when his ships encounter "the dreadful touch / Of
merchant-marring rocks" (III.ii.270–271) and his side is menaced by a
"stony adversary" (IV.i.4).

When Shylock comes on in the third scene, the easy, confident flow
of colorful talk and people is checked by a solitary figure and an
unyielding speech:

Shylock. Three thousand ducats—well.
Bassanio. Ay, sir, for three months.
Shylock. For three months—well.
Bassanio. For the which, as I told you, Antonio shall be bound.
Shylock. Antonio shall become bound—well.
Bassanio. May you stead me? Will you pleasure me? Shall I know your
     answer?
Shylock. Three thousand ducats for three months, and Antonio bound.
                                                     (I.iii.1–10)

We can construe Shylock's hesitation as playing for time while he
forms his plan. But more fundamentally, his deliberation expresses the
impersonal logic, the mechanism, involved in the control of money.
Those *well's* are wonderful in the way they bring bland Bassanio up
short. Bassanio assumes that social gestures can brush aside such con-
sideration:

Shylock. Antonio is a good man.
Bassanio. Have you heard any imputation to the contrary?
Shylock. Ho, no, no, no, no! My meaning in saying he is a good man, is
     to have you understand me that he is sufficient.   (I.iii.12–17)

The laugh is on Bassanio as Shylock drives his hard financial meaning
of "good man" right through the center of Bassanio's softer social
meaning. The Jew goes on to calculate and count. He connects the
hard facts of money with the rocky sea hazards of which we have so far
been only picturesquely aware: "ships are but boards"; and he betrays
his own unwillingness to take the risks proper to commerce: "and other
ventures he hath, squand'red abroad."

> . . . I think I may take his bond.
>
> *Bassanio.* Be assur'd you may.
>
> *Shylock.* I will be assur'd I may; and, that I may be assured, I will bethink
>   me.   (I.iii.28–31)

The Jew in this encounter expresses just the things about money which
are likely to be forgotten by those who have it, or presume they have
it, as part of a social station. He stands for what we mean when we
say that "money is money." So Shylock makes an ironic comment—and
is a comment, by virtue of his whole tone and bearing—on the folly in
Bassanio which leads him to confuse those two meanings of "good
man," to ask Shylock to dine, to use in this business context such social
phrases as "Will you *pleasure* me?" When Antonio joins them, Shylock
(after a soliloquy in which his plain hatred has glittered) becomes a
pretender to fellowship, with an equivocating mask:

> *Shylock.*   This is kind I offer.
>
> *Bassanio.* This were kindness.
>
> *Shylock.*   This kindness will I show.   (I.iii.143–144)

We are of course in no doubt as to how to take the word "kindness"
when Shylock proposes "in a merry sport" that the penalty be a pound
of Antonio's flesh.

In the next two acts, Shylock and the accounting mechanism which
he embodies are crudely baffled in Venice and rhapsodically transcended in Belmont. The solidarity of the Venetians includes the clown,
in whose part Shakespeare can use conventional blacks and whites
about Jews and misers without asking us to take them too seriously:

> To be ruled by my conscience I should stay with the Jew my master who
> (God bless the mark) is a kind of devil. . . . My master's a very Jew.
>   (II.ii.24–25,111)

Even the street urchins can mock Shylock after the passion which "the
dog Jew did utter in the streets":

> Why, all the boys in Venice follow him,
> Crying his stones, his daughter, and his ducats.   (II.viii.23–24)

Transcending Reckoning at Belmont

The simplest way to describe what happens at Belmont is to say that
Bassanio is lucky; but Shakespeare gives a great deal of meaning to his
being lucky. His choosing of the casket might be merely theatrical; but
the play's handling of the age-old story motif makes it an integral part
of the expression of relations between people and possessions. Most of

the argument about gold, silver, and lead is certainly factitious, even tedious. It must necessarily be so, because the essence of a lottery is a discontinuity, something hidden so that the chooser cannot get from here to there by reasoning. Nerissa makes explicit a primitive notion of divination:

> Your father was ever virtuous; and holy men at their death have good inspirations. Therefore the lott'ry that he hath devised in these three chests of gold, silver, and lead, whereof who chooses his meaning chooses you, will no doubt never be chosen by any rightly but one who shall rightly love.   (I.ii.30–36)

The elegant phrasing does not ask us to take the proposition very seriously, but Nerissa is pointing in the direction of a mystery. Part of the meaning is that love is not altogether a matter of the will, however willing. Portia recognizes this even when her heart is in her mouth as Bassanio is about to choose:

> Away then! I am lock'd in one of them.
> If you do love me, you will find me out.
> Nerissa and the rest, stand all aloof.
> Let music sound while he doth make his choice . . .   (III.ii.40–43)

The song, "Tell me, where is fancy bred," serves to emphasize the break, the speechless pause while Bassanio chooses. The notion that it serves as a signal to warn Bassanio off gold and silver is one of those busy-body emendations which eliminate the dramatic in seeking to elaborate it. The dramatic point is precisely that there is no signal: "Who chooseth me must give and hazard all he hath" (II.vii.16).

If we look across for a moment at Shylock, thinking through opposites as the play's structure invites us to do, his discussion with Antonio about the "thrift" of Jacob and the taking of interest proves to be relevant to the luck of the caskets. Antonio appeals to the principle that interest is wrong because it involves no risk:

> This was a venture, sir, that Jacob serv'd for;
> A thing not in his power to bring to pass,
> But sway'd and fashion'd by the hand of heaven.   (I.iii.92–94)

One way to get a fortune is to be fortunate: the two words fall together significantly at the conclusion of the opening scene:

> *Bassanio.* O my Antonio, had I but the means
> To hold a rival place with one of them,
> I have a mind presages me such thrift
> That I should questionless be fortunate!
> *Antonio.* Thou know'st that all my fortunes are at sea . . .   (I.i.173–177)

Antonio's loan is venture capital. It fits with this conception that Bassanio, when at Belmont he goes "to my fortune and the caskets," turns away from money, from "gaudy gold, / Hard food for Midas," and from silver, the "pale and common drudge / 'Tween man and man" (III.ii.101–104). Money is not used to get money; that is the usurer's way:

> *Antonio.* Or is your gold and silver ewes and rams?
> *Shylock.* I cannot tell; I make it breed as fast.   (I.iii.96–97)

Instead Bassanio's borrowed purse is invested in life—including such lively things as the "rare new liveries" (II.ii.117) that excite Launcelot, and the "gifts of rich value" which excite Nerissa to say

> A day in April never came so sweet
> To show how costly summer was at hand
> As this fore-spurrer comes before his lord.   (IIiix.93–95)

With the money, Bassanio invests *himself*, and so risks losing himself —as has to be the case with love. (Antonio's commitment of his body for his friend is in the background.) It is a limitation of the scene where he makes his choice that the risk has to be conveyed largely by the poetry, since the outward circumstances are not hazardous. Portia describes Bassanio as

> young Alcides when he did redeem
> The virgin tribute paid by howling Troy
> To the sea monster. . . . Go, Hercules!
> Live thou, I live.   (III.ii.55–61)

Of course we know that these are lover's feelings. But the moment of choice is expressed in terms that point beyond feelings to emphasize discontinuity; they convey the experience of being lost and giddily finding oneself again in a new situation. The dramatic shift is all the more vividly rendered in the language since gesture here can do little. Portia speaks of an overwhelming ecstasy of love when "all the other passions fleet to air" (III.ii.108). Bassanio likens himself to an athlete.

> Hearing applause and universal shout,
> Giddy in spirit, still gazing in a doubt
> Whether those peals of praise be his or no.   (III.ii.143–145)

He describes in a wonderful way the experience of being disrupted by joy:

> Madam, you have bereft me of all words,
> Only my blood speaks to you in my veins;

> And there is such confusion in my powers
> As, after some oration fairly spoke
> By a beloved prince, there doth appear
> Among the buzzing pleased multitude,
> Where every something, being blent together,
> Turns to a wild of nothing, save of joy,
> Express'd and not express'd.   (III.ii.175–183)

This poetry is remarkable for the conscious way that it describes being carried beyond expression, using words to tell of being beyond them. The lines in which Portia gives herself and her possessions to Bassanio make explicit, by an elaborate metaphor of accounting, that what is happening sets the accounting principle aside:

> You see me, Lord Bassanio, where I stand,
> Such as I am. Though for myself alone
> I would not be ambitious in my wish
> To wish myself much better, yet for you
> I would be trebled twenty times myself,
> A thousand times more fair, ten thousand times more rich,
> That, only to stand high in your account,
> I might in virtues, beauties, livings, friends,
> Exceed account. But the full sum of me
> Is sum of nothing which, to term in gross,
> Is an unlesson'd girl, unschool'd, unpractic'd. . . .   (III.ii.149–159)

This is extravagant, and extravagantly modest, as fits the moment; but what is telling is the way the lines move from possessions, through the paradox about sums, to the person in the midst of them all, "where I stand," who cannot be added up. It is she that Bassanio has won, and with her a way of living for which his humanity, breeding, and manhood can provide a center:

> Happiest of all is that her gentle spirit
> Commits itself to yours to be directed,
> As from her lord, her governor, her king.   (III.ii.163–165)

The possessions *follow* from this human, social relation.

Comical/Menacing Mechanism in Shylock

But the accounting mechanism which has been left behind by Bassanio and Portia has gone on working, back at Venice, to put Antonio at Shylock's mercy, and the anxiety it causes has to be mastered before the marriage can be consummated,

> For never shall you lie by Portia's side
> With an unquiet soul.   (III.ii.305–306)

Historical changes in stock attitudes have made difficulties about Shylock's role as a butt, not so much in the theater, where it works perfectly if producers only let it, but in criticism, where winds of doctrine blow sentiments and abstractions about. The Elizabethans almost never saw Jews except on the stage, where Marlowe's Barabas was familiar. They did see *one,* on the scaffold, when Elizabeth's unfortunate physician suffered for trumped-up charges of a poisoning plot. The popular attitude was that to take interest for money was to be a loan shark—though limited interest was in fact allowed by law. An aristocrat who like Lord Bassanio ran out of money commanded sympathy no longer felt in a middle-class world. Most important of all, suffering was not an absolute evil in an era when men sometimes embraced it deliberately, accepted it as inevitable, and could watch it with equanimity. Humanitarianism has made it necessary for us to be much more thoroughly insulated from the human reality of people if we are to laugh at their discomfiture or relish their suffering. During the romantic period, and sometimes more recently, the play was presented as a tragi-comedy, and actors vied with one another in making Shylock a figure of pathos. I remember a very moving scene, a stock feature of romantic productions, in which George Arliss came home after Bassanio's party, lonely and tired and old, to knock in vain at the door of the house left empty by Jessica. How completely unhistorical the romantic treatment was, E. E. Stoll demonstrated overwhelmingly in his essay on Shylock in 1911, both by wide-ranging comparisons of Shylock's role with others in Renaissance drama and by analysis of the *optique du théâtre.*

To insert a humanitarian scene about Shylock's pathetic homecoming prevents the development of the scornful amusement with which Shakespeare's text presents the miser's reaction in Solanio's narrative:

> I never heard a passion so confus'd,
> So strange, outrageous, and so variable,
> As the dog Jew did utter in the streets.
> "My daughter! O my ducats! O my daughter!
> Fled with a Christian! O my Christian ducats! . . ."   (II.viii.12–16)

Marlowe had done such a moment already with Barabas hugging in turn his money bags and his daughter—whom later the Jew of Malta poisons with a pot of porridge, as the Jew of Venice later wishes that Jessica "were hears'd at my foot, and the ducats in her coffin" (III.i.93–94). But the humanitarian way of playing the part develops suggestions that are *also* in Shakespeare's text:

> I am bid forth to supper, Jessica.
> There are my keys. But wherefore should I go?
> I am not bid for love; they flatter me.
> But yet I'll go in hate, to feed upon
> The prodigal Christian.   (II.v.11–15)

Shakespeare's marvelous creative sympathy takes the stock role of Jewish usurer and villain and conveys how it would feel to be a man living inside it. But this does not mean that he shrinks from confronting the evil and the absurdity that go with the role; for the Elizabethan age, to understand did not necessarily mean to forgive. Shylock can be a thorough villain and yet be allowed to express what sort of treatment has made him what he is:

> You call me misbeliever, cutthroat dog,
> And spet upon my Jewish gaberdine,
> And all for use of that which is mine own.   (I.iii.112–114)

We can understand his degradation and even blame the Antonios of Venice for it; yet it remains degradation:

> Thou call'dst me dog before thou hadst a cause;
> But, since I am a dog, beware my fangs.   (III.iii.6–7)

Shylock repeatedly states, as he does here, that he is only finishing what the Venetians started. He can be a drastic ironist, because he carries to extremes what is present, whether acknowledged or not, in their silken world. He insists that money is money—and they cannot do without money either. So too with the rights of property. The power to give freely, which absolute property confers and Antonio and Portia so splendidly exhibit, is also a power to refuse, as Shylock so logically refuses:

> You have among you many a purchas'd slave,
> Which, like your asses and your dogs and mules,
> You use in abject and in slavish parts,
> Because you bought them. Shall I say to you,
> "Let them be free, marry them to your heirs! . . ."
>   You will answer,
> "The slaves are ours." So do I answer you.
> The pound of flesh which I demand of him
> Is dearly bought, 'tis mine, and I will have it.   (IV.i.90–100)

At this point in the trial scene, Shylock seems a juggernaut that nothing can stop, armed as he is against a pillar of society by the principles of society itself: "If you deny me, fie upon your law! . . . I stand for judgement. Answer. Shall I have it." Nobody does answer him here, directly; instead there is an interruption for Portia's entrance. To answer him is the function of the whole dramatic action, which is making a distinction that could not be made in direct, logical argument.

Let us follow this dramatic action from its comic side. Shylock is comic, so far as he is so, because he exhibits what should be human, degraded into mechanism. The reduction of life to mechanism goes with the miser's wary calculation, with the locking up, with the preoccupation with "that which is mine own." Antonio tells Bassanio that

> My purse, my person, my extremest means
> Lie all unlock'd to your occasions.   (I.i.138–139)

How open! Antonio has to live inside some sort of rich man's melancholy, but at least he communicates with the world through outgoing Bassanio (and, one can add, through the commerce which takes his fortunes out to sea). Shylock, by contrast, who breeds barren metal, wants to keep "the vile squeeling of the wryneck'd fife" out of his house, and speaks later, in a curiously revealing, seemingly random illustration, of men who "when the bagpipe sings i'th'nose, / Cannot contain their urine" (IV.i.49–50). Not only is he closed up tight inside himself, but after the first two scenes, we are scarcely allowed by his lines to feel with him. And we never encounter him alone; he regularly comes on to join a group whose talk has established an outside point of view towards him. This perspective on him does not exclude a potential pathos. There is always potential pathos, behind, when drama makes fun of isolating, anti-social qualities. Indeed, the process of *making fun* of a person often works by exhibiting pretensions to humanity so as to show that they are inhuman, mechanical, not validly appropriate for sympathy. With a comic villain such as Shylock, the effect is mixed in various degrees between our responding to the mechanism as menacing and laughing at it as ridiculous.

So in the great scene in which Solanio and Salerio taunt Shylock, the potentiality of pathos produces effects which vary between comedy and menace:

> *Shylock.* You knew, none so well, none so well as you, of my daughter's flight.
> *Salerio.* That's certain. I, for my part, knew the tailor that made the wings she flew withal.   (III.i.27–30)

Shylock's characteristic repetitions, and the way he has of moving ahead through similar, short phrases, as though even with language he was going to use only what was his own, can give an effect of concentration and power, or again, an impression of a comically limited, isolated figure. In the great speech of self-justification to which he is goaded by the two bland little gentlemen, the iteration conveys the energy of anguish:

> —and what's his reason? I am a Jew. Hath not a Jew eyes? Hath not a Jew hands, organs, dimensions, senses, affections, passions? fed with the same food, hurt with the same weapons, subject to the same diseases, healed by the same means, warmed and cooled by the same winter and summer as a Christian is? If you prick us, do we not bleed? If you tickle us, do we not laugh? If you poison us, do we not die? And if you wrong us, shall we not revenge? If we are like you in the rest, we will resemble you in that.   (III.i.60–71)

Certainly no actor would deliver this speech without an effort at pathos; but it is a pathos which, as the speech moves, converts to menace. And the pathos is qualified, limited, in a way which is badly falsified by humanitarian renderings that open all the stops at "Hath not a Jew hands, etc. . . ." For Shylock thinks to claim only a *part* of humanness, the lower part, physical and passional. The similar self-pitying enumeration which Richard II makes differs significantly in going from "live with bread like you" to social responses and needs, "Taste grief, / Need friends" (*R.II* III.ii.175–176). The passions in Shylock's speech are conceived as reflexes; the parallel clauses draw them all towards the level of "tickle . . . laugh." The same assumption, that the passions and social responses are mechanisms on a par with a nervous tic, appears in the court scene when Shylock defends his right to follow his "humor" in taking Antonio's flesh:

> As there is no firm reason to be rend'red
> Why he cannot abide a gaping pig,
> Why he a harmless necessary cat,
> Why he a woollen bagpipe—but of force
> Must yield to such inevitable shame
> As to offend himself, being offended;
> So can I give no reason, nor I will not,
> More than a lodg'd hate and a certain loathing
> I bear unto Antonio . . .   (IV.i.52–61)

The most succinct expression of this assumption about man is Shylock's response to Bassanio's incredulous question:

> *Bassanio.* Do all men kill the things they do not love?
> *Shylock.* Hates any man the thing he would not kill?
>
>   (IV.i.66–67)

There is no room in this view for mercy to come in between "wrong us" and "shall we not revenge?" As Shylock insists, there is Christian example for him: the irony is strong. But the mechanism of stimulus and response is only a part of the truth. The reductive tendency of Shylock's metaphors, savagely humorous in Iago's fashion, goes with this speaking only the lower part of the truth. He is not cynical in Iago's aggressive way, because as an alien he simply doesn't participate in many of the social ideals which Iago is concerned to discredit in self-justification. But the two villains have the same frightening, ironical power from moral simplification.

Shylock becomes a clear-cut butt at the moments when he is himself caught in compulsive, reflexive responses, when instead of controlling mechanism he is controlled by it: "O my daughter! O my ducats!" At the end of the scene of taunting, his menace and his pathos become ridiculous when he dances like a jumping jack in alternate joy and sorrow as Tubal pulls the strings:

Tubal. Yes, other men have ill luck too. Antonio, as I heard in Genoa—
Shylock. What, what, what? Ill luck, ill luck?
Tubal. Hath an argosy cast away coming from Tripolis.
Shylock. I thank God, I thank God!—Is it true? is it true?
Tubal. I spoke with some of the sailors that escaped the wrack.
Shylock. I thank thee, good Tubal. Good news, good news! Ha, ha! Where? in Genoa?
Tubal. Your daughter spent in Genoa, as I heard, one night fourscore ducats.
Shylock. Thou stick'st a dagger in me. I shall never see my gold again. Fourscore ducats at a sitting! Fourscore ducats!
Tubal. There came divers of Antonio's creditors in my company to Venice that swear he cannot choose but break.
Shylock. I am very glad of it. I'll plague him; I'll torture him. I am glad of it.
Tubal. One of them show'd me a ring that he had of your daughter for a monkey.
Shylock. Out upon her! Thou torturest me, Tubal. It was my turquoise; I had it of Leah when I was a bachelor. I would not have given it for a wilderness of monkeys.
Tubal. But Antonio is certainly undone.
Shylock. Nay, that's true, that's very true.   (III.i.102–130)

This is a scene in the dry manner of Marlowe, Jonson, or Molière, a type of comedy not very common in Shakespeare: its abrupt alternations in response convey the effect Bergson describes so well in *Le Rire,* where the comic butt is a puppet in whom motives have become mechanisms that usurp life's self-determining prerogative. Some critics have left the rhythm of the scene behind to dwell on the pathos of the ring he had from Leah when he was a bachelor. It is like Shakespeare once to show Shylock putting a gentle sentimental value on something, to match the savage sentimental value he puts on revenge. There *is* pathos; but it is being fed into the comic mill and makes the laughter all the more hilarious.

The Community Setting Aside Its Machinery

In the trial scene, the turning point is appropriately the moment when Shylock gets caught in the mechanism he relies on so ruthlessly. He narrows everything down to his roll of parchment and his knife: "Till thou canst rail the seal from off my bond . . ." (IV.i.139). But two can play at this game:

> as thou urgest justice, be assur'd
> Thou shalt have justice more than you desir'st.   (IV.i.315–316)

Shylock's bafflement is comic, as well as dramatic, in the degree that we now see through the threat that he has presented, recognizing it to have been, in a degree, unreal. For it is unreal to depend so heavily on legal form, on fixed verbal definition, on the mere machinery by which human relations are controlled. Once Portia's legalism has broken through his legalism, he can only go on the way he started, weakly asking "Is that the law?" while Gratiano's jeers underscore the comic symmetry:

> A Daniel still say I, a second Daniel!
> I thank thee, Jew, for teaching me that word.   (IV.i.340–341)

The turning of the tables is not, of course, simply comic, except for the bold, wild and "skipping spirit" of Gratiano. The trial scene is a species of drama that uses comic movement in slow motion, with an investment of feeling such that the resolution is in elation and relief colored by amusement, rather than in the evacuation of laughter. Malvolio, a less threatening kill-joy intruder, is simply laughed out of court, but Shylock must be ruled out, with jeering only on the side lines. The threat Shylock offers is, after all, drastic, for legal instruments, contract, property are fundamental. Comic dramatists often choose to set them hilariously at naught; but Shakespeare is, as usual, scrupulously responsible to the principles of social order (however factitious his "law" may be literally). So he produced a scene which exhibits the limitations of legalism. It works by a dialectic that carries to a more general level what might be comic reduction to absurdity. To be tolerant, because we are all fools; to forgive, because we are all guilty—the two gestures of the spirit are allied, as Erasmus noted in praising the sublime folly of following Christ. Shylock says before the trial "I'll not be made a soft and dull-ey'd fool" by "Christian intercessors" (III.iii.14–15). Now when he is asked how he can hope for mercy if he renders none, he answers: "What judgement shall I dread, doing no wrong?" As the man who will not acknowledge his own share of folly ends by being more foolish than anyone else, so Shylock, who will not acknowledge a share of guilt, ends by being more guilty—and more foolish, to judge by results. An argument between Old Testament legalism and New Testament reliance on grace develops as the scene goes forward. (Shylock's references to Daniel in this scene, and his constant use of Old Testament names and allusions, contribute to the contrast.) Portia does not deny the bond—nor the law behind it; instead she makes such a plea as St. Paul made to his compatriots:

> Therefore, Jew,
> Though justice be thy plea, consider this—
> That, in the course of justice, none of us
> Should see salvation. We do pray for mercy,
> And that same prayer doth teach us all to render
> The deeds of mercy.   (IV.i.197–202)

Mercy becomes the word that gathers up everything we have seen the Venetians enjoying in their reliance on community. What is on one side an issue of principles is on the other a matter of social solidarity: Shylock is not one of the "we" Portia refers to, the Christians who say in the Lord's Prayer "Forgive us our debts as we forgive our debtors." All through the play the word Christian has been repeated, primarily in statements that enforce the fact that the Jew is outside the easy bonds of community. Portia's plea for mercy is a sublime version of what in less intense circumstances, among friends of a single communion, can be conveyed with a shrug or a wink:

> Dost thou hear, Hal? Thou knowest in the state of innocency Adam fell; and what should poor Jack Falstaff do in the days of villany?
>   (*1 H.IV* III.iii.185–188)

Falstaff, asking for an amnesty to get started again, relies on his festive solidarity with Hal. Comedy, in one way or another, is always asking for amnesty, after showing the moral machinery of life getting in the way of life. The machinery as such need not be dismissed—Portia is very emphatic about not doing that. But social solidarity, resting on the buoyant force of a collective life that transcends particular mistakes, can set the machinery aside. Shylock, closed off as he is, clutching his bond and his knife, cannot trust this force, and so acts only on compulsion:

> *Portia.*   Do you confess the bond?
> *Antonio.* I do.
> *Portia.*   Then must the Jew be merciful.

Shylock. On what compulsion must I? Tell me that.
Portia. The quality of mercy is not strain'd;
    It droppeth as the gentle rain from heaven
    Upon the place beneath. It is twice blest—
    It blesseth him that gives, and him that takes.   (IV.i.181–187)

It has been in giving and taking, beyond the compulsion of accounts,
that Portia, Bassanio, Antonio have enjoyed the something-for-nothing
that Portia here summarizes in speaking of the gentle rain from heaven.

Sharing in the Grace of Life

The troth-plight rings which Bassanio and Gratiano have given
away are all that remain of plot to keep the play moving after the trial.
It is a slight business, but it gives the women a teasing way to relish the
fact that they have played the parts of men as they give up the liberty
of that disguise to become wives. And the play's general subject is continued, for in getting over the difficulty, the group provides one final
demonstration that human relationships are stronger than their outward signs. Once more, Bassanio expresses a harassed perplexity about
obligations in conflict; and Portia gayly pretends to be almost a Shylock
about this lover's bond, carrying the logic of the machinery to absurd
lengths before showing, by the new gift of the ring, love's power to set
debts aside and begin over again.

No other comedy, until the late romances, ends with so full an
expression of harmony as that which we get in the opening of the final
scene of *The Merchant of Venice*. And no other final scene is so completely without irony about the joys it celebrates. The ironies have
been dealt with beforehand in baffling Shylock; in the moment of relief
after expelling an antagonist, we do not need to look at the limitations
of what we have been defending. So in *Summer's Last Will and Testament,* when Summer is confronted by a miserly Christmas, he comes
out wholeheartedly for festivity, whereas elsewhere, confronting spokes-
men for festivity, he is always wry about it. He dismisses Christmas with

    Christmas, I tell thee plain, thou art a snudge,
    And wer't not that we love thy father well,
    Thou shouldst have felt what 'longs to Avarice.
    It is the honor of nobility
    To keep high days and solemn festivals—
    Then to set their magnificence to view,
    To frolic open with their favorites,
    And use their neighbors with all courtesy,

> When thou in hugger-mugger spend'st thy wealth.
> Amend thy manners, breathe thy rusty gold:
> Bounty will win thee love, when thou art old:

The court compels Shylock to breathe his gold and give bounty to Lorenzo. He is plainly told that he is a snudge—and we are off to noble magnificence and frolic at Belmont. No high day is involved, though Shakespeare might easily have staged the solemn festival due after Portia's wedding. Instead Lorenzo and Jessica feel the harmony of the universe and its hospitality to life in a quiet moment of idle talk and casual enjoyment of music. There is an opening out to experience in their exquisite outdoor poetry which corresponds to the openness stressed by Nashe in contrast to miserly hugger-mugger.

> The moon shines bright. In such a night as this,
> When the sweet wind did gently kiss the trees
> And they did make no noise—in such a night
> Troilus methinks mounted the Troyan walls
> And sigh'd his soul towards the Grecian tents,
> Where Cressid lay that night.   (V.i.1–6)

The openness to experience, the images of reaching out towards it, or of welcoming it, letting music "creep in our ears," go with the perception of a gracious universe such as Portia's mercy speech invoked:

> How sweet the moonlight sleeps upon this bank!
> Here will we sit and let the sounds of music
> Creep in our ears. Soft stillness and the night
> Become the touches of sweet harmony.
> Sit, Jessica. Look how the floor of heaven
> Is thick inlaid with patens of bright gold.
> There's not the smallest orb which thou behold'st
> But in his motion like an angel sings . . .   (V.i.54–61)

Lorenzo is showing Jessica the graciousness of the Christian world into which he has brought her; and it is as richly golden as it is musical! Jessica is already at ease in it, to the point of being able to recall the pains of famous lovers with equanimity, rally her lover on his vows and turn the whole thing off with "I would out-night you did no body come, / But hark, I hear the footing of a man." That everybody is so perfectly easy is part of the openness:

Lorenzo. Who comes so fast in silence of the night?
Messenger. A friend.
Lorenzo. A friend? What friend? Your name, I pray you, friend? . . .

Sweet soul, let's in, and there expect their coming.
And yet no matter. Why should we go in?
. . . bring your music forth into the air.   (V.i.25–27, 51–54)

As the actual music plays, there is talk about its Orphic power, and
we look back a moment toward Shylock

> The man that hath no music in himself
> Nor is not mov'd with concord of sweet sounds,
> Is fit for treasons, stratagems, and spoils . . .   (V.i.82–84)

A certain contemplative distance is maintained by talking *about* perception, *about* harmony and its conditions, even while enjoying it.
Portia comes on exclaiming how far the candle throws its beams, how
much sweeter the music sounds than by day. There are conditions,
times and seasons, to be observed; but the cosmological music, which
cannot be heard directly at all, is behind the buoyant decorum of the
people:

> How many things by season season'd are
> To their right praise and true perfection!
> Peace ho! The moon sleeps with Endymion
> And would not be awak'd.   (V.i.107–110)

At the end of the play, there is Portia's news of Antonio's three argosies
richly come to harbor, and the special deed of gift for Lorenzo—
"manna in the way / Of starved people." Such particular happy events
are not sentimental because Shakespeare has floated them on an expression of a tendency in society and nature which supports life and
expels what would destroy it.

I must add, after all this praise for the way the play makes its distinction about the use of wealth, that *on reflection,* not when viewing
or reading the play, but when thinking about it, I find the distinction,
as others have, somewhat too easy. While I read or watch, all is well,
for the attitudes of Shylock are appallingly inhuman, and Shakespeare
makes me feel constantly how the Shylock attitude rests on a lack of
faith in community and grace. But when one thinks about the Portia-
Bassanio group, not in opposition to Shylock but alone (as Shakespeare
does not show them), one can be troubled by their being so very very
far above money:

> What, no more?
> Pay him six thousand, and deface the bond.
> Double six thousand and then treble that . . .
> (III.ii.298–300)

It would be interesting to see Portia say no, for once, instead of always yes: after all, Nashe's miser has a point, *"Liberalitas liberalitate perit."* One can feel a difficulty too with Antonio's bland rhetorical question:

> when did friendship take
> A breed of barren metal of his friend? (I.iii.134–135)

Elizabethan attitudes about the taking of interest were unrealistic: while Sir Thomas Gresham built up Elizabeth's credit in the money market of Antwerp, and the government regulated interest rates, popular sentiment continued on the level of thinking Antonio's remark reflects. Shakespeare's ideal figures and sentiments are open here to ironies which he does not explore. The clown's role just touches them when he pretends to grumble

> We were Christians enow before, e'en as many as could well live by one another. This making of Christians will raise the price of hogs.
>
> (III.v.23–26)

In a later chapter we shall see, in *As You Like It*, a more complete confronting of ironies, which leaves, I feel, a cleaner aftertaste. Shakespeare could no doubt have gone beyond the naïve economic morality of Elizabethan popular culture, had he had an artistic need. But he did not, because in the antithetical sort of comic form he was using in this play, the ironical function was fulfilled by the heavy contrasts embodied in Shylock.

About Shylock, too, there is a difficulty which grows on reflection, a difficulty which may be felt too in reading or performance. His part fits perfectly into the design of the play, and yet he is so alive that he raises an interest beyond its design. I do not think his humanity spoils the design, as Walter Raleigh and others argued, and as was almost inevitable for audiences who assumed that to be human was to be ipso-facto good. But it is true that in the small compass of Shylock's three hundred and sixty-odd lines, Shakespeare provided material that asks for a whole additional play to work itself out. Granville-Barker perceptively summarizes how much there is in the scene, not sixty lines long, in which Shylock is seen at home:

> The parting with Launcelot: he has a niggard liking for the fellow, is even hurt a little by his leaving, touched in pride, too, and shows it childishly.
>
> > Thou shalt not gormandize
> > As thou hast done with me . . .
>
> . . . The parting with Jessica, which we of the audience know to be a parting indeed; that constant calling her by name, which tells us of the

lonely man! He has looked to her for everything, has tasked her hard, no doubt; he is her jailer, yet he trusts her, and loves her in his extortionate way. Uneasy stranger that he is within these Venetian gates; the puritan, who, in a wastrel world, will abide by law and prophets!

To have dramatized "he has looked to her for everything, has tasked her hard, no doubt," would have taken Shakespeare far afield indeed from the prodigal story he was concerned with—as far afield as *King Lear*. Yet the suggestion is there. The figure of Shylock is like some secondary figure in a Rembrandt painting, so charged with implied life that one can forget his surroundings. To look sometimes with absorption at the suffering, raging Jew alone is irresistible. But the more one is aware of what the play's whole design is expressing through Shylock, of the comedy's high seriousness in its concern for the grace of community, the less one wants to lose the play Shakespeare wrote for the sake of one he merely suggested.

Biblical Allusion and Allegory in
The Merchant of Venice

by Barbara K. Lewalski

Perhaps no other play in the Shakespeare canon has provoked greater controversy regarding its fundamental moral and religious attitudes than has *The Merchant of Venice* [*MV*]. As everyone knows, acrimonious critical debates have long been waged concerning whether Shakespeare's attitude in the play is humanitarian or antisemitic, whether Shylock is presented as the persecuted hero or as a crude monster and comic butt, whether Antonio and Bassanio are portrayed as worthy Christians or as crass hypocrites.

Recently, however, some critics have in part transcended the controversies arising out of the literal story by concentrating upon certain allegorical and symbolic aspects of the play, reflecting in this approach the modern critical emphasis upon Shakespeare's use of Christian themes and imagery and his debt to the medieval tradition. In a most illuminating essay, Nevill Coghill [1] discusses several of Shakespeare's comedies, including *MV*, in terms of the medieval comic form described by Dante—a beginning in troubles and a resolution in joy, reflecting the fundamental pattern of human existence in this world. Moreover, he traces in *MV* the direct influence of the medieval allegorical theme of the "Parliament of Heaven," in which Mercy and Justice, two of the four "daughters of God," argue over the fate of mankind after his fall. In somewhat similar vein, Sir Israel Gollancz [2] sees the play as Shakespeare's largely unconscious development of certain myths implicit in the original sources—the myth of the Parliament of Heaven,

"Biblical Allusion, and Allegory in The Merchant of Venice*"* by Barbara K. Lewalski. From Shakespeare Quarterly, *Vol. XIII (1962), 327–43. Copyright © 1962 by the Shakespeare Association of America. Reprinted by permission of Barbara K. Lewalski and the Shakespeare Association of America.*

[1] "The Basis of Shakespearean Comedy," *Essays and Studies* III (London, 1950), pp. 1–28. See also Northrop Frye, "The Argument of Comedy," *English Institute Essays,* 1948 (N. Y., 1949), pp. 58–73.

[2] *Allegory and Mysticism in Shakespeare,* reports of lectures edited by A. W. Pollard (London, 1931), pp. 13–68.

and the related Redemption myth in which Antonio represents Christ, Shylock, Evil, and Portia, Mercy and Grace. These suggestions shed considerable light upon the trial scene, but they hardly provide a comprehensive account of the entire play.[3] The question of the extent and manner in which allegory may organize the total work has yet to be investigated, and constitutes the subject of the present inquiry.

The overingenuity and the religious special pleading that has marred some "Christian" criticism of Shakespeare make manifest the need for rigorous standards of evidence and argument in such investigations. The present study does not claim that all of Shakespeare's plays approach as closely as *MV* appears to do the themes and methods of the morality play. Nor does it imply anything about Shakespeare's personal religious convictions, since the religious significances dealt with in the play are basic to all the major Christian traditions and were available to any Elizabethan through countless sermons, biblical commentaries, and scripture annotations. Nor, again, does it assume Shakespeare's direct contact with medieval allegory, since the general Elizabethan assimilation and perpetuation of this tradition is clearly evidenced in Spenser, Marlowe, and many other poets. The study does, however, uncover in *MV* patterns of Biblical allusion and imagery so precise and pervasive as to be patently deliberate; it finds, moreover, that such language clearly reveals an important theological dimension in the play and points toward consistent and unmistakable allegorical meanings.

The allegorical aspects of *The Merchant of Venice* can, I believe, be greatly illuminated by the medieval allegorical method exemplified by Dante. Indeed, though it omits *MV*, a recent study by Bernard Spivack has persuasively argued the utility of the Dante comparison in comprehending the allegorical origins and characteristics of many Shakespearian villains.[4] In contrast to personification allegory wherein a particular is created to embody an insensible, Dante's symbolic method causes a particular real situation to suggest a meaning or meanings beyond itself. In *MV* Shakespeare, like Dante, is ultimately concerned with the nature of the Christian life, though as a dramatist he is fully as interested in the way in which the allegorical dimensions enrich the particular instance as in the use of the particular to point to higher levels of meaning. The various dimensions of allegorical significance in *MV*, though not consistently maintained throughout the play and not susceptible of analysis with schematic rigor, are generally analogous to Dante's four levels of allegorical meaning: a literal or story level; an

[3] As J. R. Brown points out, "Introduction," *The Merchant of Venice*, Arden edition (London, 1955), p. li. All subsequent references to the text are to this edition.
[4] *Shakespeare and the Allegory of Evil: the History of a Metaphor in Relation to his Major Villains* (N. Y., 1958), pp. 50–99.

Biblical Allusion and Allegory *in* The Merchant of Venice   35

a whole and to Christ as head of humanity; a moral or tropological
level dealing with factors in the moral development of the individual;
and an anagogical significance treating the ultimate reality, the Heavenly City.[5] Moreover, comprehension of the play's allegorical meanings
leads to a recognition of its fundamental unity, discrediting the common critical view that it is a hotchpotch which developed contrary to
Shakespeare's conscious intention.

The use of Biblical allusion to point to such allegorical meanings
must now be illustrated in relation to the various parts of the work.

Antonio and Shylock

At what would correspond in medieval terminology to the "moral"
level, the play is concerned to explore and define Christian love and
its various antitheses.[6] As revealed in the action, Christian love involves
both giving and forgiving: it demands an attitude of carelessness regarding the things of this world founded upon a trust in God's providence; an attitude of self-forgetfulness and humility founded upon
recognition of man's common sinfulness; a readiness to give and risk
everything, possessions and person, for the sake of love; and a willingness to forgive injuries and to love enemies. In all but the last respect,
Antonio is presented throughout the play as the very embodiment of
Christian love, and Shylock functions as one (but not the only) anti-
thesis to it.

Antonio's practice of Christian love is indicated throughout the play
under the metaphor of "venturing," and the action begins with the use
of this metaphor in a mock test of his attitude toward wealth and
worldly goods. The key scripture text opposing love of this world to
the Christian love of God and neighbor is Matt. vi.19–21,31–33:

Lay not up treasures for your selves upon the earth, where the moth and
canker corrupt, & where theeves dig through and steale./ But lay up treas-

[5] H. Flanders Dunbar, *Symbolism in Medieval Thought* (New Haven, 1929), pp. 19,
497. Cf. Dante, "Letter to Can Grande della Scala," in *Dante's Eleven Letters,* ed. G.
R. Carpenter (N. Y., 1892).

[6] Many critics have suggested that the play is essentially concerned with the contrast and evaluation of certain moral values—such as money, love, and friendship;
appearance and reality; true love and fancy; mercy and justice; generosity and possessiveness; the usury of commerce and the usury of love. See Brown, Arden ed., pp.
xxxvii–lviii; M. C. Bradbrook, *Shakespeare and Elizabethan Poetry* (London, 1951),
pp. 170–179; Cary B. Graham, "Standards of Value in the *Merchant of Venice,"
Shakespeare Quarterly,* IV (N. Y., 1953), 145–151; C. R. Baskervill, "Bassanio as an
Ideal Lover," *Manly Anniversary Studies,* pp. 90–103. All these, however, may be sub-
sumed under the central concern, Christian Love.

ures for your selves in heaven. . . ./ For where your treasure is, there will
your heart be also/ . . . . Therefore take no thought, saying, what shall
we eate? or what shall we drink? or wherewith shall we be clothed?/ . . .
But seeke ye first the kingdome of God, and his righteousnesse, & all these
things shalbe ministred unto you.[7]

In language directly alluding to this passage, Salario suggests that Antonio's melancholy may result from worry about his "ventures" at sea:
"Your mind is tossing on the ocean,/ There where your argosies [are],"
and Solanio continues in this vein: "had I such venture forth,/ The
better part of my affections would/ Be with my hopes abroad"
(I.i.8–9,15–17).[8] Gratiano repeats the charge—"You have too much
respect upon the world:/ They lose it that do buy it with much care"
(I.i.74–75)—a speech also recalling Matt. xvi.25–26, "Whosoever will
save his life, shall lose it. . . ./ For what shall it profite a man, though
he should winne the whole worlde, if he lose his owne soule?" Yet the
validity of Antonio's disclaimer, "I hold the world but as the world
Gratiano" (I.i.77)—that is, as the world deserves to be held—is soon
evident: his sadness is due not to worldly concern but to the imminent
parting with his beloved friend Bassanio. After witnessing this parting
Salerio testifies, "I think he only loves the world for him" (II.viii.50).

Gratiano's second playful charge, that Antonio's melancholy may be
a pose to feed his self-importance, to seem a "Sir Oracle" with a wise
and grave demeanor (I.i.88–102), recalls the passage in 1 Cor. xiii.4–5
where Paul characterizes Christian love in terms of humility and self-
forgetfulness: "Love suffereth long: it is bountifull: love envieth not:
love doth not boast it selfe: it is not puffed up:/ It disdaineth not: it
seeketh not her owne things." But this charge against Antonio is
quickly dismissed by Bassanio as "an infinite deal of nothing" (I.i.114–
118).

The quality of Antonio's love is then shown in the positive forms of
charity and benevolence, according to the following requirements of
scripture:

[7] Unless otherwise indicated, scripture quotations are from the *Geneva Bible* (London, 1584; 1st ed., 1560). Richmond Noble, *Shakespeare's Biblical Knowledge* (London, 1935), notes that all of Shakespeare's Biblical allusions are drawn from one or
more of the following versions—*Geneva, Geneva-Tomson* (1st ed., 1576), and the
Bishops Bible (1st ed., 1568), and that the first two, being quartos, had the widest
circulation during the period. For this play, the Geneva renderings seem on the
whole closest, though occasionally the phraseology suggests that of the *Bishops Bible,*
which Shakespeare may have recalled from the church services.

[8] In these speeches they testify to their own failure to come up to the standard of
Christian perfection achieved by Antonio. Shylock's later speech concerning Antonio's
"sufficiency" also alludes to the imagery of this Biblical passage in describing the
transiency of worldly goods: "Ships are but boards, sailors but men, there be land-
rats, and water-rats, water-thieves and land-thieves" (I. iii. 19–21).

> Give to every man that asketh of thee: and of him that taketh away thy goods, aske them not againe./ And if ye lende to them of whom yee hope to receive, what thanke shal ye have? for even the sinners lend to sinners, to receive the like./ Wherefore . . . doe good, & lend, looking for nothing againe, and your reward shall be great (Luke vi.30,34–35).
>
> Greater love then this hath no man, then any man bestoweth his life for his friendes (John xv.13).

Though his first loan to Bassanio has not been repaid, Antonio is willing to "venture" again for his friend "My purse, my person, my extremest means" (I.i.138), even to the pledge of a pound of his flesh. And when this pledge (and with it his life) is forfeit, he can still release Bassanio from debt: "debts are clear'd between you and I" (III.ii.317). Furthermore, Antonio lends money in the community at large without seeking interest, and often aids victims of Shylock's usurious practices (I.iii.39–40; III.iii.22–23).

Shylock's "thrift" poses the precise contrast to Antonio's "ventures." His is the worldliness of niggardly prudence, well-characterized by his avowed motto, "Fast bind, fast find,—/ A proverb never stale in thrifty mind" (II.v.53–54). He locks up house and stores before departing, he begrudges food and maintenance to his servant Launcelot, he demands usurious "assurance" before lending money. This concern with the world poisons all his relations with others and even his love for Jessica: the confused cries, "My daughter! O my ducats! O my daughter!" after Jessica's departure (II.viii.15), reveal, not his lack of love for his daughter, but his laughable and pitiable inability to determine what he loves most. Shylock also manifests pride and self-righteousness. He scorns Antonio's "low simplicity" in lending money gratis (I.iii.38–39), despises the "prodigal" Bassanio for giving feasts (II.v.15), and considers the "shallow fopp'ry" of the Christian maskers a defilement of his "sober house" (II.v.35–36).

The moral contrast of Shylock and Antonio is more complex with reference to that most difficult injunction of the Sermon on the Mount —forgiveness of injuries and love of enemies. Recollection of this demand should go far to resolve the question as to whether an Elizabethan audience would regard Shylock's grievances as genuine:[9] presumably an audience which could perceive the Biblical standard

[9] For the argument that Shylock could have been nothing but a monster and comic butt to an Elizabethan audience steeped in antisemitism, see E. E. Stoll, *Shakespeare Studies* (N. Y., 1927), pp. 255–336. This argument has been challenged on the ground that there was little ordinary antisemitism in England in Shakespeare's time, because few Jews resided there, and also on the ground that Shylock is, for a part of the play at least, made human, complex, and somewhat sympathetic. See H. R. Walley, "Shakespeare's Portrayal of Shylock," *The Parrott Presentation Volume* (Princeton, N. J., 1935), pp. 211–242, and J. L. Cardozo, *The Contemporary Jew in Elizabethan Drama* (Amsterdam, 1926).

operating throughout the play would also see its relevance here. (The text is Matt. v.39,44–47):

> Resist not evill: but whosoever shall smite thee on thy right cheeke, turn to him the other also/ . . . . Love your enemies: bless them that curse you: do good to them that hate you, and pray for them which hurt you, and persecute you./ That ye may be the children of your Father that is in heaven: for hee maketh his sunne to arise on the evill, & the good, and sendeth raine on the just, and unjust./ For if ye love them, which love you, what reward shall you have? Doe not the Publicanes even the same?/ And if ye be friendly to your brethren onely, what singular thing doe ye? doe not even the Publicanes likewise?

Antonio at the outset of the play is rather in the position of the publican described as friendly to his brethren only—he loves and forgives Bassanio beyond all measure, but hates and reviles Shylock.[10] For evidence of this we have not only Shylock's indictment, "You call me misbeliever, cut-throat dog,/ And spet upon my Jewish gaberdine,/ . . . And foot me as you spurn a stranger cur" (I.iii.106–107,113), but also Antonio's angry reply promising continuation of such treatment: "I am as like to call thee so again, / To spet on thee again, to spurn thee too" (I.iii.125–126). Indeed, the moral tension of the play is lost if we do not see that Shylock, having been the object of great wrongs, must make a difficult choice between forgiveness and revenge—and that Antonio later finds himself in precisely the same situation.

Ironically, Shylock poses at first as the more "Christian" of the two in that, after detailing his wrongs, he explicitly proposes to turn the other cheek—to "Forget the shames that you have stain'd me with,/ Supply your present wants, and take no doit/ Of usance for my moneys" (I.iii.135–137). Of course it is merely pretence: Shylock had declared for revenge at the first sight of Antonio (I.iii.41–42), and, according to Jessica's later report, he eagerly planned for the forfeit of Antonio's flesh long before the bond came due (III.ii. 283–287). And in this fixed commitment to revenge, this mockery of forgiveness, lies I believe the reason for the often-deplored change from the "human" Shylock of the earlier scenes to the "monster" of Act IV. At the level of the moral allegory Shylock undergoes (rather like Milton's Satan) the progressive deterioration of evil; he turns by his own choice into the cur that he has been called—"Thou call'dst me dog before thou hadst a cause, / But since I am a dog, beware my fangs" (III.iii.6–7). Conversely, Antonio in the trial scene suffers hatred and injury but foregoes revenge and rancor, manifesting a genuine

---

[10] Hence Shylock's reference to Antonio as a "Fawning publican" may allude to the passage cited above (Matt. v.47) as well as, more obviously, to the parable of the Pharisee and the Publican.

spirit of forgiveness—for Shylock's forced conversion is not revenge, as will be seen. Thus, his chief deficiency surmounted, Antonio becomes finally a perfect embodiment of Christian love.

The Shylock-Antonio opposition functions also at what the medieval theorists would call the "allegorical" level; in these terms it symbolizes the confrontation of Judaism and Christianity as theological systems —the Old Law and the New—and also as historic societies. In their first encounter, Shylock's reference to Antonio as a "fawning publican" and to himself as a member of the "sacred nation" (I.iii.36,43) intro- duces an important aspect of this contrast. The reference is of course to the parable of the Pharisee and the Publican (Luke xviii.9–13) which was spoken "unto certayne which trusted in themselves, that they were ryghteous, and despised other." [11] Shylock's words are evi- dently intended to suggest the Pharisee's prayer, "God I thank thee that I am not as other menne are, extorcioners, unjust, adulterers, or as this Publicane: / I fast twyce in the weeke, I geve tythe of al that I posesse," and his scornful reference to Antonio's "low simplicity" relates Antonio to the Publican who prayed with humble faith, "God be merciful to me a sinner." The contemporary interpretation of this parable is suggested in Tomson's note: [12] "Two things especially make our prayers voyde and of none effect: confidence of our owne ryghteous- nesse, and the contempts of other. . . . we [are] despised of God, as proude & arrogant, if we put never so little trust in our owne workes before God." Through this allusion, then, the emphasis of the Old Law upon perfect legal righteousness is opposed to the tenet of the New Law that righteousness is impossible to fallen man and must be replaced by faith—an opposition which will be further discussed with reference to the trial scene.

Also in this first encounter between Antonio and Shylock, the argu- ment about usury contrasts Old Law and New in terms resembling those frequently found in contemporary polemic addressed to the usury question. Appealing to the Old Testament, Shylock sets forth an analogy between Jacob's breeding of ewes and rams and the breed- ing of money to produce interest. [13] Antonio, denying the analogy with the query, "is your gold and silver ewes and rams?" echoes the com- monplace Christian argument (based upon Aristotle) [14] that to take

[11] *Bishops Bible* (London, 1572).

[12] *The New Testament. . . .* Englished by L. Tomson (London, 1599).

[13] Again they refer to their characteristic metaphors: Shylock argues that Jacob's trick to win the sheep from Laban (Gen. xxx.31–43) was justifiable "thrift," whereas Antonio (citing a later verse, Gen. xxxi.9, referring the trick to God's inspiration) declares that it was rather a "venture . . . / A thing not in his power to bring to pass, / But sway'd and fashion'd by the hand of heaven."

[14] *Politics,* I.10. 1258ᵇ. 1–8. Cf. Francis Bacon, "Of Usury," *Essays* (1625), "They say . . . it is against Nature, for *Money* to beget *Money*."

interest is to "breed" barren metal, which is unnatural. Antonio's remark, "If thou wilt lend this money, lend it not/ As to thy friends, for when did friendship take/ A breed for barren metal of his friend?/ But lend it rather to thine enemy" (I.iii.127–130), prescribes Shylock's course of action according to the dictum of the Old Law— "Unto a stranger thou mayest lend upon usury, but unto thy brother thou shalt not lend upon usury" (Deut. xxiii.20). However, according to most exegetes, the Gospel demanded a revision of this rule. Aquinas declares, "The Jews were forbidden to take usury from their brethren, i.e., from other Jews. By this we are given to understand that to take usury from any man is evil simply, because we ought to treat every man as our neighbor and brother, especially in the state of the Gospel, whereto all are called." [15] Furthermore, the Sermon on the Mount was thought to forbid usury absolutely by the words, "Lend, looking for nothing againe," a text which is glossed as follows in the Geneva Bible—lend, "not only not hoping for profite, but to lose ye stocke, and principall, for as much as Christ bindeth him selfe to repaie the whole with a most liberall interest."

At this same encounter, Shylock's pretense of following the Christian prescription regarding forgiveness of injuries again contrasts Old Law and New as theological systems, for it recalls the fact that Christ in the Sermon on the Mount twice opposed the Christian standard to the Old Law's demand for strict justice: "Ye have heard that it hath bene saide, An eye for an eye, & a tooth for a tooth./[16] But I say unto you, Resist not evill: but whosoever shall smite thee on thy right cheeke, turne to him the other also / . . . Ye have hearde that it hath bene saide, Thou shalt love thy neighbour, & hate thine enemie. / But I say unto you, Love your enemies" (Matt. v.38–39,43–44). Later, some of the language of the trial scene alludes again to the differing demands of the two dispensations with regard to forgiveness of enemies:

> *Bass:* Do all men kill the things they do not love?
> *Shy:* Hates any man the thing he would not kill?
> *Bass:* Every offense is not a hate at first!
> *Shy:* What! wouldst thou have a serpent sting thee twice?   (IV.i.66–69)

And the Duke reiterates this opposition almost too pointedly when he

[15] *Summa Theologica* II-II, Ques. 78, Art. 1, in *The Political Ideas of St. Thomas Aquinas,* ed. Dino Bigongiari (N. Y., 1953), p. 149. As R. H. Tawney points out in *Religion and the Rise of Capitalism* (N. Y., 1953), p. 135, the arguments of the schoolmen were in constant circulation during the sixteenth century, and the medieval view regarding usury was maintained by an overwhelming proportion of Elizabethan writers on the subject (pp. 128–149). See Sir Thomas Wilson, *Discourse upon Usury* (1572), Miles Mosse, *The Arraignment and Conviction of Usurie* (1595), H. Smith, *Examination of Usury* (1591).

[16] Christ refers to Exod. xxi.24; Levit. xxiv.20; Deut. xix.21.

tenders Shylock the mercy of the Christian court, observing that Shylock could recognize from this "the difference of our spirit" (IV.i.364).

This allegorical dimension encompasses also the historical experience of the two societies, Jewish and Christian. After Jessica's departure, Shylock explicitly assumes unto himself the sufferings of his race: "The curse never fell upon our nation till now, I never felt it till now (III.i.76–78). This curse is that pronounced upon Jerusalem itself— "Behold, your habitation shalbe left unto you desolate" (Matt.xxiii.38). First Shylock's servant Launcelot leaves the "rich Jew" to serve the poor Bassanio; then his daughter Jessica[17] "gilds" herself with her Father's ducats and flees with her "unthrift" Christian lover; and finally, all of Shylock's goods and his very life are forfeit to the state. Shylock's passionate outcries against Antonio (III.i.48 ff.) also take on larger than personal significance: they record the sufferings of his entire race in an alien Christian society—"he hath disgrac'd me . . . laugh'd at my losses, mock'd at my gains, scorned my nation, thwarted my bargains, cooled my friends, heated mine enemies—and what's his reason? I am a Jew!" This is followed by the eloquent plea for recognition of the common humanity Jew shares with Christian, "Hath not a Jew eyes? . . . ." and it concludes with the telling observation that despite the Christian's professions about "humility" and turning the other cheek, in practice he is quick to revenge himself upon the Jew. The taunts of Salario, Solanio, and Gratiano throughout the play give some substantiation to these charges.

Yet overlaying this animosity are several allusions to Shylock's future conversion, suggesting the Christian expectation of the final, premillennial conversion of the Jews. The first such reference occurs, most appropriately, just after Shylock's feigned offer to forego usury and forgive injury. Antonio salutes Shylock's departure with the words,

---

[17] It has been plausibly argued that Jessica's name derives from the Hebrew Jesca, a form of Iscah, daughter of Haran (Gen. xi.29), glossed by Elizabethan commentators as "she that looketh out" (Gollancz, p. 42, G. L. Kittredge ed., *Merchant of Venice*, Ginn, 1945, p. ix). A direct play upon this name seems to occur in II.v.31–32, where Shylock directs Jessica, "Clamber not you up to the casements then / Nor thrust your head into the public street," and Launcelot prompts her to "look out at window for all this (II.v.40) to see Lorenzo. Her departure thus signifies a breaking out of the ghetto, a voluntary abandonment of Old Law for New. This significance is continued in III.v.1–5, when Launcelot quips that Jessica will be damned since (according to Mosaic Law, Exod. xx.5) the "sins of the father are to be laid upon the children," and she replies (ll.17–18), "I shall be sav'd by my husband"—reecting Paul's promise in the New Law, 1 Cor. vii.14, "the unbeleeving wife is sanctified by the husband." Shylock's name is probably taken from Shalach, translated by "Cormorant" (Levit. xi.17, Deut. xiv.17)—an epithet often applied to usurers in Elizabethan English. The name "Tubal," taken from Tubal Cain (Gen. x.2,6) is glossed in Elizabethan Bibles as meaning "worldly possessions, a bird's nest of the world" (Gollancz, pp. 40–41; Kittredge, p. ix).

"Hie thee gentle Jew"—probably carrying a pun on gentle-gentile—
and then prophesies, "The Hebrew will turn Christian, he grows kind"
(I.iii.173–174). "Kind" in this context implies both "natural" (in fore-
going unnatural interest) and "Charitable"; thus Antonio suggests that
voluntary adoption of these fundamental Christian principles would
lead to the conversion of the Jew. The second prediction occurs in
Lorenzo's declaration, "If e'er the Jew her father come to heaven, / It
will be for his gentle daughter's sake" (II.iv.33–34)—again with the
pun on gentle-gentile. As Shylock's daughter and as a voluntary convert to Christianity, Jessica may figure forth the filial relationship of
the New Dispensation to the Old, and Lorenzo's prediction may carry
an allusion to Paul's prophecy that the Jews will ultimately be saved
through the agency of the Gentiles.[18] At any rate, the final conversion
of the Jews is symbolized in just such terms in the trial scene: because
Antonio is able to rise at last to the demands of Christian love, Shylock
is not destroyed, but, albeit rather harshly, converted. Interestingly
enough, however, even after Portia's speeches at the trial have reminded
Antonio and the court of the Christian principles they profess, Gratiano
yet persists in demanding revenge. This incident serves as a thematic
counterpoint to the opposition of Old Law and New, suggesting the
disposition of Christians themselves to live rather according to the Old
Law than the New. Such a counterpoint is developed at various points
throughout the play—in Antonio's initial enmity to Shylock, in the
jeers of the minor figures, in Shylock's statements likening his revenge
to the customary vengeful practices of the Christians and his claim to
a pound of flesh to their slave trade in human flesh (IV.i.90–100). Thus
the play does not present arbitrary, black-and-white moral estimates of
human groups, but takes into account the shadings and complexities
of the real world.

As Shylock and Antonio embody the theological conflicts and historical interrelationships of Old Law and New, so do they also reflect,
from time to time, the ultimate sources of their principles in a further
allegorical significance. Antonio, who assumes the debts of others (res-
cuing Bassanio, the self-confessed "Prodigal," from a debt due under
the law) reflects on occasion the role of Christ satisfying the claim of
Divine Justice by assuming the sins of mankind. The scripture phrase
which Antonio's deed immediately brings to mind points the analogy
directly: "This is my commandment, that ye love one another, *as I
have loved you. /*[19] Greater love hath no man than this, that a man
lay down his life for his friends" (John xv.12–13). And Shylock, demanding the "bond" which is due him under the law, reflects the role

---

[18] See Richard Hooker's paraphrase of this prophecy, *Of the Laws of Ecclesiastical
Polity* Bk. V, Appen. I, *Works,* ed. John Keble (Oxford, 1845), II, 587–588.
[19] Italics mine.

of the devil, to whom the entire human race is in bondage through sin—an analogy which Portia makes explicit when she terms his hold upon Antonio a "state of hellish cruelty." The dilemma which that delightful malaprop Launcelot experiences with regard to leaving Shylock, whom he terms the "devil incarnation" (II.ii.1–30), springs directly from the implications of this analogy. According to 1 Pet. xii.18–19, one must serve even a bad master "for conscience toward God": thus Launcelot's conscience bids him stay and the fiend bids him go. But on the other hand, to serve the devil is obviously damnation; so he concludes, "in my conscience, my conscience is but a kind of hard conscience to offer to counsel me to stay with the Jew," and determines flight. Similarly, Jessica declares, "Our house is hell" (II.iii.2), thus placing her departure in the context of a flight from the devil to salvation. As E. E. Stoll points out,[20] the identification of Jew and Devil is repeated nine times in the play, and was a commonplace of medieval and Elizabethan antisemitic literature. Yet it seems to function here less to heap opprobrium upon the Jew than to suggest the ultimate source of the principles of revenge and hatred which Shylock seeks to justify out of the Law. Again the meaning is clarified by a Biblical quotation—Christ's use of the same identification in denouncing the Jews for their refusal to believe in him and their attempts to kill him—"Ye are of your father the devill, and the lustes of your father ye will doe: Hee hath bene a murtherer from the beginning" (John viii.44).

Bassanio and the Caskets

The story of Bassanio and the casket choice also appears to incorporate a "moral" and an "allegorical" meaning. At the moral level, the incident explores the implications of Christian love in the romantic relationship, whereas Antonio's story deals with Christian love in terms of friendship and social intercourse. Morocco, in renouncing the leaden casket because it does not offer "fair advantages," and in choosing the gold which promises "what many men desire," exemplifies the confusion of love with external shows:[21] like most of the world, he values Portia not for herself but for her beauty and wealth. However, the death's head within the golden casket indicates the common mortality to which all such accidents as wealth and beauty are finally subject.

[20] *Shakespeare Studies,* pp. 270–271.
[21] Morocco amusingly displays the illogic in his own position. He begs that he be not judged by his tawny complexion but rather by his valor and inner worth (II.i. 1–12), and then argues that the picture symbolic of Portia could be fittingly placed only in a golden casket (II.vii.48–55).

Aragon, by contrast, represents love of self so strong that it precludes any other love. He renounces the gold because he considers himself superior to the common multitude whom it attracts; he disdains the lead as not "fair" enough to deserve his hazard; and in choosing the silver which promises "as much as he deserves" he declares boldly, "I will assume desert" (II.ix.51). But the blinking idiot in the casket testifies to the folly of him who supposes that love can be bargained for in the pitiful coin of human merit. Bassanio, on the other hand, chooses the lead casket which warns, "Who chooseth me, must give and hazard all he hath" (II.ix.21)—thus signifying his acceptance of the self-abnegation, risk, and venture set up throughout the play as characteristics of true Christian love. And the metaphor of the "venture" is constantly used with reference to Bassanio and Portia just as it is with Antonio. Bassanio proposes to venture like a Jason for the golden fleece of Portia's sunny locks (I.i.169–177), and, though Portia complains that it is hard to be subject to the lottery of the caskets, she accepts the premise that this hazard will reveal her true lover (I.ii. 12–34; III.ii.41). Finally, when Bassanio goes forth to choose she likens his venture, upon which her own fate depends, to that of Hercules striving to rescue Hesione from the sea-monster:[22] "I stand for sacrifice, / The rest aloof are the Dardanian wives, / With bleared visages come forth to view / The issue of th'exploit: go Hercules" (III.ii.57–60).

At the "allegorical" level, the caskets signify everyman's choice of the paths to spiritual life or death. This analogy is explicitly developed in the "Moral" appended to the casket story in the *Gesta Romanorum* which is almost certainly Shakespeare's source for this incident.[23] In the *Gesta* the casket choice tests the worthiness of a maiden (the soul) to wed the son of an Emperor (Christ). The moral declares, "The Emperour sheweth this Mayden three vessells, that is to say, God putteth before man life & death, good and evill, & which of these he chooseth hee shall obtaine." [24] This passage contains a reference to Deut. xxx.15–20, wherein Moses warns, after delivering the commandments to the Jews:

> Beholde, I have set before thee this day life and good, death and evill/ . . . But if thine heart turne away, so that thou wilt not obey, but shalt be seduced and woorship other gods, and serve them,/ I pronounce unto you this day, that ye shall surely perish. . . ./ Therefore chuse life, that both

[22] Interestingly, Morocco also compares the casket choice to an exploit of Hercules, but not to one fairly testing strength and true worth, as does Portia. Rather, he sees it as a dice game wherein by pure chance Hercules might loose out to his valet (II. l. 31–34).
[23] A selection of stories from the *Gesta* was printed in English translation by Richard Robinson in 1577 and again in 1595. See Arden *MV,* pp. xxxii, 172–174.
[24] Arden *MV,* p. 174.

thou and thy seede may live./ By loving the Lord thy God, by obeying his voyce, and by cleaving unto hym: For he is thy life, & the length of thy dayes: that thou mayest dwell in the lande which the Lord sware unto thy fathers.

As a note in the Bishops Bible indicates, the last promise was taken to refer not only to the "land of Chanaan, but also the heavenly inheritance, whereof the other was a figure." That Shakespeare intended to recall this Biblical allusion so pointed in the *Gesta,* and thus to make the caskets symbolize the great choices of spiritual life and death, is evident by the constant references in the lovers' conversation to "life" and "death" just before Bassanio's venture. Bassanio declares, "Let me choose, / For as I am, I live upon the rack"; Portia continues the "rack" metaphor, urging, "Confess and live," a phrase which Bassanio immediately transposes to "Confess and Love" (III.ii. 24–35). When he goes forth to venture, Portia calls for music to celebrate whichever result, death or life, will attend his choice: "If he lose he makes a swan-like end, / Fading in music" into the "wat'ry deathbed" of her tears. If he win, music will celebrate his Hercules-like victory and the life of both—"Live thou, I live." That the casket choice represents Everyman's choice among values is further emphasized by the multitude at Portia's door: some of them refuse to choose (like the inhabitants of the vestibule of Hell in Dante); others choose wrongly and, having demonstrated by this that they are already wedded to false values, are forbidden to make another marriage. Furthermore, Antonio's action in making possible Bassanio's successful venture reflects the role of Christ in making possible for the true Christian the choice of spiritual life, the love of God.

The meaning of the symbolic caskets is further illuminated by James v.2–3: "Your riches are corrupt: and your garments are moth-eaten. / Your golde and silver is cankred, and the rust of them shall be a witness against you." [25] Morocco, the pagan, with his boasts of bravery in battle and of the love of the "best-regarded virgins of our clime," with his sensuous imagery and dashing superlatives (II.i.1–38) is a fit type of worldliness, Mammon. The warning of the death's head is that such a life is spiritual death: "Many a man his life had sold / But my outside to behold,—/ Gilded tombs do worms infold." Aragon, the Spaniard—the very embodiment of Pride according to the Elizabethan caricature—is the type of Pharisaical self-righteousness: his sonorously complacent language about the "barbarous multitudes" and the faults of others (II.ix.19–52) rather suggests the "sounding brasse" and "tinckling cymbale" of Paul's image (1 Cor. xiii.1), and certainly recalls

[25] The same imagery appears in Matt. vi.25, the passage alluded to in testing Antonio's contempt for worldly goods (p. 329 above).

the Pharisee's prayer. But through its first line, "The fire seven times tried this," the scroll refers Aragon to the twelfth Psalm,[26] which denounces vanity and proud speaking. It then refers to the casket as merely "silver'd o'er"—thus suggesting Christ's comparison of the scribes and pharisees to "whited sepulchres" (Matt. xxiii.27). Also, the blinking idiot within the casket mutely testifies that since all men are sinners pharisaical pride is folly.[27] This defeat and lessoning of Morocco and Aragon foreshadows the defeat and conversion of Shylock, for he represents in somewhat different guise these same antichristian values of worldliness and self-righteousness.[28]

Bassanio's choice of the lead casket is the choice of life, the love of God. The use of romantic love as a symbol for divine love is of course a commonplace in mystical literature, deriving chiefly from the example of the Song of Solomon, which was understood to treat, as the caption in the Bishops Bible expresses it, "The familiar talke and mystical communication of the spiritual love between Jesus Christe and his Churche." Bassanio's meditation on the caskets (III.ii.73–107) symbolically suggests his understanding and renunciation of the two kinds of "Ornament" which oppose this love: his description of the silver as "thou common drudge between man and man" suggests his knowledge of the pretense of righteousness with which men generally cover their vices when presenting themselves to others, and the skull image which he uses in denouncing the gold indicates his awareness of the transience and corruptibility of worldly goods. Also clarifying the significance of Bassanio's choice is Portia's remark, "I stand for sacrifice," made in relation to her Hercules-Hesione simile as she sends Bassanio forth to choose (III.ii.57). The word "stand" is ambiguous, suggesting at once that she occupies the position of a sacrificial victim whose life must be saved by another, but also that she "represents" sacrifice—the very core of Christian love. The exact counterpart of Portia's remark, both in form and ambiguity of meaning, is Shylock's later comment, "I stand for judgment. . . . I stand here for law" (IV.i.103,142).

[26] Psalter for the *Book of Common Prayer,* in *Bishops Bible,* 1584, verses 3, 7: "The Lorde shal roote out al deceptful lippes: and the tongue that speaketh proude thinges / . . . . The woordes of the Lord are pure woordes: even as the silver whiche from the earth is tryed, and purified seven times in the fyre."

[27] The *Gesta's* moral points to the same meanings though the inscriptions on the caskets are somewhat different: the gold is said to represent "worldly men, both mightie men & riche, which outwardly shine as golde in riches and pomps of this world," the silver stands for "some Justices & wise men of this world which shine in faire speach but within they be full of wormes and earth"—as were the whited sepulchres (Arden *MV,* Appendix V, p. 174; Cf. Matt. xxiii.24).

[28] Aragon's appeal to Portia after his defeat, "Did I deserve no more than a fool's head? / Is that my prize? are my deserts no better" (II.ix.59–60), foreshadows Portia's role in the trial scene as opponent and judge of the claim based upon righteousness.

The Trial

The trial scene climaxes the action at all the levels of meaning that have been established. As has been suggested, it portrays at the moral level Shylock's degradation to a cur and a monster through his commitment to revenge, and by contrast, Antonio's attainment of the fullness of Christian love through his abjuration of revenge. Allegorically, the scene develops the sharpest opposition of Old Law and New in terms of their respective theological principles, Justice and Mercy, Righteousness and Faith; it culminates in the final defeat of the Old Law and the symbolic conversion of the Jew.

Throughout the first portion of Act IV, until Portia begins the dramatic reversal with the words, "Tarry a little, there is something else—" (IV.i.301), the action is simply a debate between Old Law and New in terms of Justice and Mercy—but that debate is carried forth in a dual frame of reference. The phrase in the Lord's Prayer rendered by both the Bishops and the Geneva Bibles as "Forgeve us our dettes, as we forgeve our detters," is alluded to twice in this scene, making the debtor's trial in the court of Venice a precise analogue of the sinner's trial in the court of Heaven. The Duke inquires of Shylock, "How shalt thou hope for mercy rend'ring none?" (IV.i.88), and Portia reiterates, "Though justice be thy plea, consider this, / That in the course of justice, none of us / Should see salvation: we do pray for mercy, / And that same prayer, doth teach us all to render / The deeds of mercy" (IV.i.194–198). In his *Exposition of the Lord's Prayer* a contemporary clergyman, William Perkins,[29] works out a similar analogy: "For even as a debt doth binde a man, either to make satisfaction, or els to goe to prison: so our sinnes bindes us either to satisfie Gods justice, or else to suffer eternall damnation." Shylock is referred for this analogy not only to the Lord's Prayer but also to his own tradition: Portia's language (IV.i.180 ff.) echoes also certain Old Testament psalmists and prophets whose pleas for God's mercy were explained by Christian exegetes as admissions of the inadequacies of the Law and testimonies of the need for Christ.[30] For example the striking image, "Mercy . . . droppeth as a gentle rain from Heaven upon the place beneath," echoes Ecclesiasticus xxv.19, "O how fayre a thyng is mercy in the tyme of

[29] Cambridge, 1605, p. 410.

[30] See Psalms 103, 136, 143. With reference to such passages, Henrie Bullinger declares (*Fiftie Godlie and Learned Sermons*, trans. H. I., London, 1587, p. 403), "The ancient Saints which lived under the old testament, did not seeke for righteousness and salvation in the works of the lawe, but in him which is the perfectnes and ende of the law, even Christ Jesus."

anguish and trouble: it is lyke a cloud of rayne that commeth in the tyme of drought." This reference should also remind Shylock of the remarkable parallel to the Lord's Prayer contained in a passage following close upon this one: "He that seeketh vengeance, shal finde vengeance of the Lord. . . . / Forgive thy neyghbour the hurt that he hath donne thee, and so shal thy sinnes be forgeven thee also when thou prayest / . . . . He that sheweth no mercie to a man which is lyke himselfe, how dare he aske forgevenesse of his sinnes" (Ecclus. xxiii. 1–24).[31]

Through these allusions, Antonio's predicament in the courtroom of Venice is made to suggest traditional literary and iconographical presentations of the "Parliament of Heaven" in which fallen man was judged. Both sides agree that Antonio's bond (like the sinner's) is forfeit according to the law, and that the law of Venice (like that of God) cannot be abrogated. Shylock constantly threatens, "If you deny me, fie upon your law" (IV.i.101), and Portia concurs, "there is no power in Venice / Can alter a decree established" (IV.i.214–215). The only question then is whether the law must be applied with strictest justice, or whether mercy may somehow temper it. In the traditional allegory of the Parliament of Heaven,[32] Justice and Mercy, as the two principal of the four "daughters" of God, debate over the judgement to be meted out to man; Launcelot Andrewes in his version of the debate[33] aligns these figures with the Old Law and the New respectively—"Righteousnesse, she was where the Law was (for, that, the *rule* of *righteousnesse*) where the Covenant of the Old Testament was, *doe this and live* (the very voyce of Justice)," whereas "The Gentiles they claim by *Mercy,* that is their virtue." So in the trial scene Shylock as the embodiment of the Old Law represents Justice: "I stand for Judgment. . . . I stand here for Law" (IV.i.103,142), whereas Portia identifies herself with that "Quality of Mercy" enthroned by the New Law. Also, another conception of the Heavenly Court is superadded to this by means of several references during the trial to Shylock as Devil (IV.i.213,283). The scene takes on something of the significance of the trial described in the medieval drama, the *Processus Belial,* in which the Devil claims by justice the souls of mankind due him under the law, and the Virgin Mary intercedes for man by appealing to the Mercy of God.[34]

In either formulation, the demands of Justice and Mercy are reconciled only through the sacrifice of Christ, who satisfies the demands of

---

[31] *Bishops Bible.*

[32] For a resumé of this tradition see Samuel C. Chew, *The Virtues Reconciled* (Toronto, 1947).

[33] "Christmas, 1616," *XCVI Sermons,* 3rd Edn. (London, 1635), p. 104.

[34] See John D. Rea, "Shylock and the *Processus Belial,*" *PQ,* VIII (Oct., 1929), 311–313.

justice by assuming the debts of mankind, and thus makes mercy possible. Therefore it is not surprising that the courtroom scene also evokes something of the crucifixion scene—as the moment of reconciling these opposed forces, as the time of defeat for the Old Law, as the prime example of Christian Love and the object of Christian Faith. Both plot situation and language suggest a typical killing of Christ by the Jew. Antonio, baring his breast to shed his blood for the debt of another, continues the identification with Christ occasionally suggested at other points in the play. Shylock's cry, "My deeds upon my head" (IV.i.202) clearly suggests the assumption of guilt by the Jews at Christ's crucifixion—"His blood be on us, and on our children" (Matt. xxvii.25) —and his later remark, "I have a daughter— / Would any of the stock of Barrabas / Had been her husband, rather than a Christian" (IV.i. 291–293) recalls the Jews' choice of the murderer Barrabas over Christ as the prisoner to be released at Passover (Matt. xxvii.16–21). A similar fusion of the symbols of debtor's court and crucifixion occurs in a Christmas sermon by Launcelot Andrewes on Gal. iii.4–5:

> If one be in debt and danger of the *Law,* to have a *Brother* of the same bloud . . . will little avail him, except he will also come *under the Law,* that is, become his Surety, and undertake for him. And such was our estate. As debtors we were, by vertue of . . . the *handwriting* that was against us. Which was our *Bond,* and we had forfeited it. . . . Therefore Hee became bound for us also, entred bond anew, took on Him, not only our *Nature,* but our *Debt.* . . . The debt of a Capitall Law is Death.[35]

Throughout the action thus far described, Shylock has persistently denied pleas to temper justice with mercy—to forgive part of the debt, to accept three times the value of the debt rather than the pound of flesh, or even to supply a doctor "for charity" to stop Antonio's wounds. His perversity is rooted in his explicit denial of any need to "deserve" God's mercy by showing mercy to others, for he arrogates to himself the perfect righteousness which is the standard of the Old Law—"What judgment shall I dread doing no wrong?" (IV.i.89). Accordingly, after Portia's "Tarry a little," the action of the scene works out a systematic destruction of that claim of righteousness, using the laws of Venice as symbol. Shylock is shown first that he can claim nothing by the law: his claim upon Antonio's flesh is disallowed by the merest technicality. This reflects the Christian doctrine that although perfect performance of the Law would indeed merit salvation, in fact fallen man could never perfectly observe it, any more than Shylock could take Antonio's flesh without drawing blood. According to Paul, Romans iii.9–12, "all, both Jewes and Gentiles are under sinne, / . . . There is none righteous, no not one. / . . . there is none that doth good, no not one. / Therefore by the workes of the Law shal no flesh be justified in his sight." Next, Shylock is shown that in claiming the Law he not only gains nothing, but stands to lose all that he possesses and even life itself. He becomes subject to what Paul terms the "curse" of the Law, since he is unable to fulfill its conditions: "For as many as are of the workes of the Lawe, are under the curse: for it is written, Cursed is every man that continueth not in all things, which are written in the booke of the Lawe, to do them" (Gal. iii.10).

The names applied to and assumed by Portia during the trial reinforce these meanings. When Portia gives judgment at first in Shylock's favor, he cries out, "A Daniel come to judgment: yea, a Daniel! / O wise young judge," in obvious reference to the apocryphal Book of Susanna, wherein the young Daniel confounded the accusers of Susanna, upholding thereby the justice of the Law. The name, Daniel, which means in Hebrew, "The Judge of the Lord," was glossed in the Elizabethan Bibles as "The Judgment of God." [36] But the name carries other implications as well, which Shylock ironically forgets. Portia has assumed the name "Balthasar" for the purposes of her disguise, and the name given to the prophet Daniel in the Book of Daniel is Baltassar—a similarity hardly accidental.[37] According to Christian exegetes, Daniel in this book foreshadows the Christian tradition by his explicit denial of any claim upon God by righteousness, and his humble appeal for mercy: "O my God, encline thyne eare, & hearken, open thyne eyes, beholde howe we be desolated . . . for we doo not present our prayers before thee in our owne righteousnesse, but in thy great mercies" (Daniel ix.18).[38] These implications greatly enrich the irony when Gratiano flings the title back in Shylock's face—"A second Daniel, a Daniel, Jew" (IV.i.329).

Shylock's "forced conversion" (a gratuitous addition made by Shakespeare to the source story in *Il Pecorone*) must be viewed in the context of the symbolic action thus far described. Now that Shylock's claim to legal righteousness has been totally destroyed, he is made to accept the only alternative to it, faith in Christ. Paul declares (Gal. ii.16), "A man

---

[36] See glossary, *Geneva Bible*.

[37] The slight variation may be due to imperfect memory: the king whom Daniel served was named Balthasar.

[38] *Bishops Bible*. A note on this passage declares that it shows how "the godly flee only unto gods mercies and renounce theyr owne workes when they seeke for remission of their sinnes." Cf. Bullinger, *Fiftie Sermons*, p. 434: "And although they did not so usually call upon God as wee at this day doe, through the mediatour and intercessour Christe Jesus . . . yet were they not utterly ignorant of the mediatour, for whose sake they were heard of the Lord. Daniel in the ninth Chapter of his prophecie maketh his prayer, and desireth to bee hearde of God for the Lordes sake, that is, for the promised Christ his sake."

is not justified by the workes of the Lawe, but by the fayth of Jesus Christ," and a note in the Bishops Bible explains, "Christ hath ful- fylled the whole lawe, and therefore who so ever beleeveth in him, is counted just before God, as wel as he had fulfylled ye whole law him selfe." Thus the stipulation for Shylock's conversion, though it of course assumes the truth of Christianity, is not antisemitic revenge: it simply compels Shylock to avow what his own experience in the trial scene has fully "demonstrated"—that the Law leads only to death and destruc- tion, that faith in Christ must supplant human righteousness. In this connection it ought to be noted that Shylock's pecuniary punishment under the laws of Venice precisely parallels the conditions imposed upon a Jewish convert to Christianity throughout most of Europe and also in England during the Middle Ages and after. All his property and goods, as the ill-gotten gain of usury, were forfeit to the state upon his conversion, but he was customarily allotted some proportion (often half) of his former goods for his maintenance, or else given a stipend or some other means of support.[39]

There is some evidence that Shylock himself in this scene recognizes the logic which demands his conversion, though understandably he finds this too painful to admit explicitly. His incredulous question "Is that the law" (IV.i.309) when he finds the law invoked against him, shows a new and overwhelming consciousness of the defects of legalism. Also, he does not protest the condition that he become a Christian as he protested the judgment (soon reversed) which would seize all his property: his brief "I am content" suggests, I believe, not mean-spirited- ness but weary acknowledgement of the fact that he can no longer make his stand upon the discredited Law.

Indeed, Portia's final tactic—that of permitting the Law to demon- strate its own destructiveness—seems a working out of Paul's metaphor of the Law as a "Schoolemaster to bring us to Christ, that we might be made righteous by faith" (Gal. iii.24). The metaphor was utilized by all the major Christian theological traditions, and received much the same interpretation in all of them:

> The law was our pedagogue in Christ. . . . So also did he [God] wish to give such a law as men by their own forces could not fulfill, so that, while presuming on their own powers, they might find themselves to be sinners, and, being humbled, might have recourse to the help of grace. (Aquinas) [40]
>
> Another use of the law is . . . to reveale unto a man his sinne, his blind- nes, his misery, his impietie, ignoraunce, hatred and contempt of God,

[39] James Parkes, *The Jew in the Medieval Community* (London, 1938), pp. 101–146; Michael Adler, *Jews of Medieval England* (London, 1939), pp. 280–334; Cecil Roth, *A History of the Jews in England* (Oxford, 1949), p. 96.

[40] *Summa Theologica*, II.I. Ques. 98. Art. 2, in *Basic Writings,* ed. Anton Pegis (N. Y., 1944), p. 809.

death, hel, the judgment and deserved wrath of God to the end that God might bridle and beate down this monster and this madde beaste (I meane the presumption of *mans* own righteousness) . . . [and drive] them to Christ. (Luther) [41]

Some . . . from too much confidence either in their own strength or in their own righteousness, are unfit to receive the grace of Christ till they have first been stripped of every thing. The law, therefore, reduces them to humility by a knowledge of their own misery, that thus they may be prepared to pray for that of which they before supposed themselves not destitute. (Calvin) [42]

And, from the contemporary sermon literature the following commentaries are typical:

The law . . . was given because of transgression. . . . out of the which they might learn the will of God, what sin, right, or unright is; and to know themselves, to go into themselves, and to consider, how that the holy works which God requireth are not in their own power; for the which cause all the world have great need of a mediator. . . . Thus was the law our schoolmaster unto Christ. (Myles Coverdale) [43]

The law . . .shewes us our sinnes, and that without remedy: it shewes us the damnation that is due unto us: and by this meanes, it makes us despaire of salvation in respect of our selves: & thus it inforceth us to seeke for helpe out of our selves in Christ. The law is then our schoolemaster not by the plaine teaching, but by stripes and corrections. (Perkins) [44]

Thus Shylock, as representative of his entire race, having refused the earlier opportunity to embrace voluntarily the principles of Christianity, must undergo in the trial scene the harsh "Schoolmastership" of the Law, in order to be brought to faith in Christ.

The Ring Episode and Belmont

The ring episode is, in a sense, a comic parody of the trial scene—it provides a means whereby Bassanio may make at least token fulfillment of his offer to give "life itself, my wife, and all the world" (IV.i.280) to

[41] *A Commentarie of M. Doctor Martin Luther upon the Epistle of S. Paul to the Galathians* (London, Thomas Vautroullier, 1575), n.p.

[42] *Institutes of the Christian Religion,* II, Chap. 7, trans. John Allen (Philadelphia, Pa., 1936), I, 388.

[43] "The Old Faith," trans. by Myles Coverdale from H. Bullinger. 1547, *Writings and Translations,* ed. George Pearson (Cambridge, 1844), pp. 42–43.

[44] *A Commentarie, or Exposition upon the first five chapters of the Epistle to Galatians* (London, 1617), p. 200. See also, John Donne, Sermon 17, *Sermons,* ed. E. Simpson and G. Potter, VI (Berkeley, Calif., 1953), 334–345; John Colet, *An Exposition of St. Paul's Epistle to the Romans,* 1497, trans. J. H. Lupton (London, 1873), pp. 1–18.

deliver Antonio. The ring is the token of his possession of Portia and all Belmont: in offering it Portia declared, "This house, these servants, and this same myself / Are yours . . . I give them with this ring, / Which when you part from, lose, or give away, / Let it presage the ruin of your love, / And be my vantage to exclaim on you" (III.ii.170–174). So that in giving the ring to the "lawyer" Balthasar—which he does only at Antonio's bidding—Bassanio surrenders his "claim" to all these gifts, even to Portia's person, and is therefore taunted at his return with her alleged infidelity. But Belmont is the land of the spirit, not the letter, and therefore after Bassanio has been allowed for a moment to feel his loss, the whole crisis dissolves in laughter and amazement as Antonio again binds himself (his soul this time the forfeit) for Bassanio's future fidelity, and Portia reveals her own part in the affair. At the moral level, this pledge and counter pledge by Bassanio and Antonio continue the "venture" metaphor and further exemplify the willingness to give all for love. At the allegorical level, despite the lighthearted treatment, "Bassanio's comic "trial" suggests the "judgment awaiting the Christian soul as it presents its final account and is found deficient. But Love, finally, is the fulfillment of the Law and covers all defects—Bassanio's (Everyman's) love in giving up everything, in token at least, for Antonio, and Antonio's (Christ's) love toward him and further pledge in his behalf.

Belmont functions chiefly at the anagogical level (if one may invoke the term): it figures forth the Heavenly City. Jessica points to this analogy explicitly—"It is very meet / The Lord Bassanio live an upright life / For having such a blessing in his lady, / He finds the joys of heaven here on earth" (III.v.67–70). Here Gentile and Jew, Lorenzo and Jessica, are united in each other's arms, talking of the music of the spheres:

> How sweet the moonlight sleeps upon this bank! . . .
>   Look how the floor of heaven
> Is thick inlaid with patens of bright gold,
> There's not the smallest orb which thou behold'st
> But in his motion like an angel sings,
> Still quiring to the young-eye'd cherubins;
> Such harmony is in immortal souls   (V.i.54,58–63)

And Portia's allusion upon returning, "Peace!—how the moon sleeps with Endymion, / And would not be awak'd" (V.i.108–109) also suggests eternity, for Diana, enamoured of Endymion's beauty, caused him to sleep forever on Mount Latmos. In Belmont all losses are restored and sorrows end: Bassanio wins again his lady and all Belmont; Antonio is given a letter signifying that three of his argosies are returned to port richly laden; and Lorenzo receives the deed naming him Shylock's future heir. Lorenzo's exclamation, "Fair ladies, you drop manna in the way of starving people," together with the reference to "patens" in the passage quoted above, sets up an implied metaphor of the heavenly communion. Here all who have cast their bread upon the waters in the "ventures" of Christian love receive the reward promised:

> Whoever shall forsake houses, or brethren, or sisters, or father, or mother, or wife, or children, or landes, for my names sake, hee shal receive an hundreth folde more, and shal inherite everlasting life (Matt. xix:29).

The Merchant of Venice

by Harley Granville-Barker

The Merchant of Venice is a fairy tale. There is no more reality in Shylock's bond and the Lord of Belmont's will than in Jack and the Beanstalk.

Shakespeare, it is true, did not leave the fables as he found them. This would not have done; things that pass muster on the printed page may become quite incredible when acted by human beings, and the unlikelier the story, the likelier must the mechanism of its acting be made. Besides, when his own creative impulse was quickened, he could not help giving life to a character; he could no more help it than the sun can help shining. So Shylock is real, while his story remains fabulous; and Portia and Bassanio become human, though, truly, they never quite emerge from the enchanted thicket of fancy into the common light of day. Aesthetic logic may demand that a story and its characters should move consistently upon one plane or another, be it fantastic or real. But Shakespeare's practical business, once he had chosen these two stories for his play, was simply so to charge them with humanity that they did not betray belief in the human beings presenting them, yet not so uncompromisingly that the stories themselves became ridiculous.

What the producer of the play must first set himself to ascertain is the way in which he did this, the nice course that—by reason or instinct —he steered. Find it and follow it, and there need be no running on the rocks. But logic may land us anywhere. It can turn Bassanio into a heartless adventurer. Test the clock of the action by Greenwich time, it will either be going too fast or too slow. And as to Portia's disguise and Bellario's law, would the village policeman be taken in by either?

But the actor will find that he simply cannot play Bassanio as a hum-
bug, for Shakespeare does not mean him to. Portias and Nerissas
have been eclipsed by wigs and spectacles. This is senseless tomfoolery;
but how make a wiseacre producer see that if he does not already know?
And if, while Shylock stands with his knife ready and Antonio with his
bared breast, the wise young judge lifting a magical finger between
them, we sit questioning Bellario's law—why, no one concerned, actors
or audience, is for this fairyland, that is clear.

The Merchant of Venice is the simplest of plays, so long as we do not
bedevil it with sophistries. Further, it is—for what it is!—as smoothly
and completely successful, its means being as well fitted to its ends, as
anything Shakespeare wrote. He was happy in his choice of the Portia
story; his verse, which has lost glitter to gain a mellower beauty and an
easier flow, is now well attuned to such romance. The story of Shylock's
bond is good contrast and complement both; and he can now project
character upon the stage, uncompromising and complete. Yet this Shylock does not overwhelm the play, as at a later birth he might well
have done—it is a near thing, though! Lastly, Shakespeare is now
enough of the skilled playwright to be able to adjust and blend the
two themes with fruitful economy.

The Construction of the Play

The Problem of "Double-Time"

This blending of the themes would, to a modern playwright, have
been the main difficulty. The two stories do not naturally march together. The forfeiture of the bond must be a matter of months; with
time not only of the essence of the contrast, but of the dramatic effect.
But the tale of the caskets cannot be enlarged, its substance is too
fragile; and a very moderate charge of emotion would explode its
pretty hollowness altogether. Critics have credited Shakespeare with
nice calculation and amazing subtlety in his compassing of the time-
difficulty. Daniel gives us one analysis, Halpin another, Eccles a third,
and Furness finds the play as good a peg for the famous Double Time
theory as Wilson, its inventor, found Othello. All very ingenious; but
is the ingenuity Shakespeare's or their own? [1] For him dramatic time

---

[1] If the effect is one and the same, one might think the question unimportant. But
Daniel, making out his three months, is generous of "intervals," not only between
acts, but between scenes; and even Furness, on his subtler scent, can say, "One is
always conscious that between the acts of a play a certain space of time elapses. To
convey this impression is one of the purposes for which a drama is divided into acts."
Therefore an important and a much-disputed question is involved—and begged.

was a naturally elastic affair. (It still is, though less so, for the modern playwright, whose half-hour act may commonly suggest the passing of an hour or two; this also is Double Time.) Shakespeare seems to think of it quite simply in terms of effect, as he thought of dramatic space, moving his characters hither and thither without considering the compassing of yards or miles. The one freedom will imply and enhance the other. The dramatist working for the "realistic" stage must settle definitely where his characters are to be and keep them there till he chooses to change the scenery. Shakespeare need not; and, in fact, he never insists upon place at all, unless it suits him to; and then only to the extent that suits him.[2] In this play, for instance, where we find Shylock and Antonio will be Venice, but whereabouts in Venice is usually no matter; when it is—at Shylock's door or in court before the Duke—it will be made clear enough to us. And where Portia is, is Belmont. He treats time—and the more easily—with a like freedom, and a like aim. Three months suits for the bond; but once he has pouched the money Bassanio must be off to Belmont, and his calendar, attuned to his mood, at once starts to run by hours only. The wind serves, and he sails that very night, and there is no delay at Belmont. Portia would detain him some month or two before he ventures; and what could be more convenient for a Shakespeare bent on synchronizing the two stories? For that matter, he could have placed Belmont a few hundred miles off, and let the coming and going eke out the time. Did the problem as a whole ever even occur to him? If it did, he dismissed it as of no consequence. What he does is to set each story going according to its nature; then he punctuates them, so to speak, for effect. By the clock they are not even consistent in themselves, far less with each other. But we should pay just the sort of attention to these months, days or hours that we do, in another connection, to the commas and semicolons elucidating a sentence. They give us, and are meant to, simply a *sense* of time and its exactions. It is the more easily done because our own sense of time in daily life is far from consistent. Time flies when we are happy, and drags in anxiety, as poets never tire of reminding us. Shakespeare's own reflections on the phenomenon run to half a column of the concordance, and he turns it quite naturally to dramatic account.

The True Problem

How to blend two such disparate themes into a dramatically organic whole; that was his real problem. The stories, linked in the first scene,

---

And, in practice, the pernicious hanging-up of performances by these pauses is encouraged, to which scenery and its shifting is already a sufficient temptation.
    [2] See also Preface to *Antony and Cleopatra*.

will, of themselves, soon part company. Shakespeare has to run them
neck and neck till he is ready to join them again in the scene of the
trial. But the difficulty is less that they will not match each other by the
clock than that their whole gait so differs, their very nature. How is the
flimsy theme of the caskets to be kept in countenance beside its grimly
powerful rival? You cannot, as we said, elaborate the story, or charge it
with emotion; that would invite disaster. Imagine a Portia seriously
alarmed by the prospect of an Aragon or a Morocco for husband. What
sort of barrier, on the other hand, would the caskets be to a flesh-and-
blood hero and heroine fallen in love? Would a Romeo or Rosalind
give a snap of the finger for them? As it is, the very sight of Bassanio
prompts Portia to rebellion; and Shakespeare can only allow his lovers
a few lines of talk together, and that in company, dare only color the
fairy tale with a rhetorically passionate phrase or so before the choice
is made and the caskets can be forgotten—as they are!—altogether. Nor
does anything in the play show the artist's supreme tact in knowing
what *not* to do better than this?

But you cannot neglect the Portia story either, or our interest in her
may cool. Besides, this antiphony of high romance and rasping hate
enhances the effect of both. A contrasting of subjects, scene by scene, is
a trick (in no depreciatory sense) of Shakespeare's earliest stagecraft,
and he never lost his liking for it.[3] Then if the casket-theme cannot be
neglected, but cannot be elaborated, it must somehow be drawn out,
its peculiar character sustained, its interest husbanded while its con-
summation is delayed.

Shakespeare goes straightforwardly enough to work. He puts just as
little as may be into Portia's first scene; but for the one sounding of
Bassanio's name there would be only the inevitable tale of the caskets
told in tripping prose and the conventional joking upon the suitors.
Portia and Nerissa, however, seen for the first time in the flesh, give it
sufficient life, and that "Bassanio" one vivid spark more. Later, in due
course, come Morocco's choice of the gold casket and Aragon's of the
silver. We remark that Morocco is allotted two scenes instead of one.
The reason is, probably, that Shakespeare has now enriched himself
with the Lorenzo-Jessica story (not to mention the episode of the
Gobbos, father and son), and, with this extra weight in the Venetian
scale of the action, is put to it to maintain the balance. He could, of
course, finish with both Morocco and Aragon earlier and give Bassanio
two scenes instead of one.[4] And if a romantic hero could not well wait

[3] It is, one may say, a commonplace of stagecraft, Elizabethan or other; but none
the less worthy for that.
[4] And such interest as there is in Aragon's scene is now lessened, perhaps, by our
knowledge that Bassanio is on his way; even more, by the talk in the scene before of
Antonio's misfortune. But Shakespeare, as his wont is, plucks some little advantage

till after dinner to make his choice, as Morocco does, Solanio's arrival
with the ill news of Antonio could easily have been kept for the later
scene. But this will not do either—most characteristically will not do
for Shakespeare. He has held his lovers apart, since the air of the Belmont of the caskets is too rarefied for flesh and blood to breathe. And
Portia herself has been spellbound; we have only had jaunty little
Nerissa to prophesy that love (by the pious prevision of the late lord)
would somehow find out the way.[5] But once he brings them together
Bassanio must break the spell. It is the story of the sleeping beauty and
the prince in another kind; a legitimate and traditional outcome. And
once Shakespeare himself has broken free of the fairy tale and brought
these two to life (for Bassanio as well has been till now a little blood-
less) it is not in him to let them lapse from the scene unproved, and to
the full. The long restraint has left him impatient, and he must, here
and now, have his dramatic fling. We need not credit—or discredit
him, if you like—with much calculation of the problem. It was common prudence both to keep Belmont as constantly in our view as
Venice, and the emancipating Bassanio clear of it for as long as possible. And he is now in the middle of his play, rather past it, ready to
link his two stories together again. He worked forthrightly; that is
written plain over most of his work. Though he might now find that he
had here material for two scenes, he would not return in his tracks,
telescope Aragon and Morocco—and take, in fact, all the sort of
trouble we, who are his critics, must take to explain what a much more
compact job he could have made of it! Besides, here is his chance to
uplift the two as hero and heroine, and he will not dissipate its effec-
tiveness.

For Bassanio, as we said, has been till now only little less bound than
Portia in the fetters of a fairy tale; and later, Shylock and the bond

---

from the poverty of the business by capping Aragon's vapidity with the excitement
of the news of Bassanio's arrival.

[5] Though there are commentators who maintain that Nerissa—even Portia, perhaps
—gives Bassanio the hint to choose lead, or has it sung to him:

> Tell me, where is fancy *bred*,
> In the heart, or in the *head?*
> How begot, how nouri*shed?*

And if he'll only listen carefully he will note that they all rhyme with *lead*.

Shakespeare was surely of a simpler mind than this—his audiences too. And he
had some slight sense of the fitness of things. Would he—how *could* he?—wind up
this innocent fairy tale with such a slim trick? Besides, how was it to be worked;
how is an audience to be let into the secret? Are they likely to tag extra rhymes to
the words of a song as they listen to it? Or is Nerissa—not Portia, surely!—at some
point to tip Bassanio "the wink" while he smiles knowingly back to assure her that
he has "cottoned on"? Where, oh, where indeed, are such dramatic fancies bred? Not
in any head that will think out the effect of their realization.

will condemn him to protesting helplessness, and the affair of the rings
to be merrily befooled.[6] The wonder indeed is, considering the rather
poor figure—painfully poor by the gospel according to Samuel Smiles—
the coercion of the story makes him cut, that throughout he measures up
so well to the stature of sympathetic hero. Shakespeare contrives it in
two ways. He endows him with very noble verse; and, whenever he can,
throws into strong relief the Bassanio of his own uncovenanted imagination. He does this here. The fantasy of the caskets brought to its due
crisis, charged with an emotion which blows it for a finish into thin air,
he shows us Bassanio, his heart's desire won, agonized with grief and
remorse at the news of Antonio's danger. Such moments do test a man
and show him for what he is; and this one, set in bright light and made
the scene's turning point, counts for more in the effect the character
makes on us than all the gentlemanly graces of his conventional equip-
ment. Unless the actor is much at fault, we shall hear the keynote to
the true Bassanio struck in the quiet simplicity—such contrast to his
rhetoric over the caskets, even though this was less mere rhetoric than
Morocco's and Aragon's—of the speech which begins

> O sweet Portia,
> Here are a few of the unpleasant'st words
> That ever blotted paper! . . .
> Rating myself at nothing, you shall see
> How much I was a braggart. When I told you
> My state was nothing, I should then have told you
> That I was worse than nothing; for indeed
> I have engaged myself to a dear friend,
> Engaged my friend to his mere enemy,
> To feed my means. . . .

Here speaks Shakespeare's Bassanio; and it is by this, and all that will
belong to it, that he is meant to live in our minds.

Producer and actors must look carefully into the way by which in
this scene the method that has served for the casket story is resolved
into something better fitted to the theme of the bond (dominant from
the beginning of the play, and now to absorb and transform the dedi-
cated Portia and her fortunes). It is a change—though we must not
insist on the contrast more than Shakespeare does—from dramatic
convention to dramatic life. From the beginning the pulse of the scene
beats more strongly; and Portia's

[6] Little to be found in him, upon analysis, to refute the frigid verdict lately passed
upon him by that distinguished and enlightened—but in this instance, surely, most
mistakenly whimsical—critic, Sir Arthur Quiller-Couch, of fortune-hunter, hypocrite
and worse. Is anything more certain than that Shakespeare did not *mean* to present
us with such a hero? If Sir Arthur were producing the play, one pities the actor
asked to give effect to his verdict.

> I pray you, tarry: pause a day or two
> Before you hazard; for in choosing wrong,
> I lose your company; therefore forbear awhile. . . .

is not only deeper in feeling (there has been little or nothing to rouse her till now; she has had to be the picture of a Portia, hardly more, with a spice of wit to help her through), but how much simpler in expression! When Bassanio turns to those obsessing caskets she must lapse again for a space into fancies of his swanlike end, her eye the watery deathbed for him, into talk about Hercules and Alcides (borrowed, one fears, from Morocco), about Dardanian wives and the like —even as he will be conventionally sententious over his choice. But note how, within the convention, preparing an escape from it, emotion is roused and sustained. With the rhetoric of Portia's

> Go, Hercules!
> Live thou, I live: with much, much more dismay
> I view the fight, than thou that mak'st the fray.

for a springboard, the song and its music are to stir us,

> *whilst Bassanio comments on the caskets to himself.*

So (let the actor remember) when he does at last speak, the emotional ascent will have been half climbed for him already. And while he pays his tribute of trope and maxim, Portia, Nerissa and the rest watch him in silence, at full strain of attention, and help to keep us, too, intent. The speech itself sweeps unhindered to its height, and the pause while the casket is unlocked is filled and enriched by the intensity of Portia's

> How all the other passions fleet to air . . .

most cunningly contrived in meaning and melody, with its emphasis on "despair" and "ecstasy" and "excess," to hold us upwrought. The fairy tale is finally incarnate in the fantastic word-painting of the portrait and the reading of the scroll. Then, with a most delicate declension to reality, Bassanio comes to face her as in a more actual world, and the curtains can be drawn upon the caskets for the last time. Observe that not for a moment has Shakespeare played his fabulous story false. He takes his theater too seriously to go spoiling an illusion he has created. He consummates it, and turns the figures of it to fresh purpose, and they seem to suffer no change.

Throughout the scene—throughout the play, and the larger part of all Elizabethan drama for that matter—effects must be valued very much in terms of music. And, with the far adventuring of his playwriting hardly begun, Shakespeare's verse is already fairly flawless, and its maneuvering from mood to mood masterly, if still simple. We have the royal humility of the speech in which Portia yields herself (Bassanio slips back to his metaphors for a moment after this); then, for contrast, the little interlude of Gratiano and Nerissa, with the tripping monosyllables of Gratiano's

> I wish you all the joy that you can wish;
> For I am sure you can wish none from me. . . .

to mark the pace and the tone of it. Then follows the arrival of Antonio's messenger with Lorenzo and Jessica; done in plain, easy-moving verse that will not discount the distressed silence in which he reads the letter, nor the quiet candor of his confession to Portia. Now comes another crescendo—two voices added to strengthen it—leading up to her generous, wide-eyed

> What sum owes he the Jew?
> *Bassanio.* For me, three thousand ducats.
> *Portia.*   What, no more!
> Pay him six thousand, and deface the bond;
> Double six thousand, and then treble that. . . .

which itself drops to the gentleness of

> Since you are dear bought I will love you dear.

Then, to strengthen the scene's ending, we have the austere prose of Antonio's letter, chilling us to misgiving. And since—in stage practice, and with the prevailing key of the play's writing to consider—this will not do for an actual finish, there is a last modulation into the brisk coda of

> Since I have your good leave to go away,
> I will make haste: but till I come again,
> No bed shall e'er be guilty of my stay,
> Nor rest be interposer 'twixt us twain.

   Lorenzo and Jessica make another link (though their relation to Belmont is pretty arbitrary) between the two stories. This, however, is but the secondary use of them. There must be a sense of time passing in Venice while the bond matures, yet we must have continuous action there, too, while the ritual at Belmont goes its measured way; so, as there can be little for Shylock and Antonio to do but wait, this third, minor theme is interposed. It brings fresh impetus to the action as well as new matter; and it shows us—very usefully—another and more human side of Shylock. Shakespeare does not scheme it out overcarefully. The masking and the elopement and the coming and going they involve are rather inconveniently crowded together (the pleasant episode of the Gobbos may have stolen a little necessary space); and one chapter of the story—for were we perhaps to have seen Shylock at supper with Bassanio, Lorenzo and the rest while the disguised Jessica waited on them?—was possibly crowded out altogether.

Once the fugitives, with some disregard of likelihood, have been brought to Belmont, Gobbo in attendance, Shakespeare turns them to account quite shamelessly. They play a mighty poor scene to give Portia and Nerissa time to disguise themselves as doctor and clerk.[7] They will have to play another while doctor and clerk change to Portia and Nerissa again; but for that, as if in compensation, they are to be dowered with the loveliest lines in the play.[8] With the junction of the themes in the trial-scene the constructive problem is, of course, solved. Shylock disappearing, the rest is simple.

SHAKESPEARE'S VENICE

If Lorenzo and Jessica and a little poetry and the consort of music, which no well-regulated great household of his time would be without, are Shakespeare's resources (he had no other; and what better should we ask?) for the painting of the starlit garden of Belmont at the play's end, for its beginning he must show us Venice. He troubles with no verbal scene-painting here; throughout the first scene the very word is but spoken twice, and quite casually. We might be anywhere in the city, or out of it, even. Therefore we hear of the Rialto, of a gondola, of the common ferry and suchlike incidentals; but of the picturesque environment to which modern staging has accustomed us there is no suggestion at all. Yet he does present a Venice that lived in the Elizabethan mind, and it is the Venice of his dramatic needs; a city of royal merchants trading to the gorgeous East, of Jews in their gaberdines (as rare a sight, remember, as to us a Chinese mandarin is, walking the London streets today), and of splendid gentlemen rustling in silks. To the lucky young Englishman who could hope to travel there Venice stood for culture and manners and the luxury of civilization; and this—without one word of description—is how Shakespeare pictures it.

We are used nowadays to see the play begun by the entry of a depressed, sober-suited, middle-aged man and two skipping youths, who

[7] Possible extra time was needed for the shifting of the caskets and their furniture and the setting of the chairs of state for the Duke and the Magnificoes. But in that case these last must have been very elaborate.

[8] For the bearing of this upon the question of act-division, see p. 364. [The reference is not to the present volume but to the volume from which this essay is reprinted, where Granville-Barker restates his belief that the dialogue between Lorenzo and Jessica at the beginning of V.i. is to allow Portia and Nerissa to change their garments. Editor's note.]

make their way with a sort of desperate merriment through such lines as the producer's blue pencil has left them, vanish shamefacedly, reappear at intervals to speak the remnant of another speech or two, and slip at last unregarded into oblivion. These are Solanio and Salarino, cursed by actors as the two worst bores in the whole Shakespearean canon; not excepting, even, those other twin brethren in nonentity, Rosencrantz and Guildenstern.[9] As characters, Shakespeare has certainly not been at much pains with them; they could exchange speeches and no one would be the wiser, and they move about at everybody's convenience but their own. But they have their use, and it is an important one; realize it, and there may be some credit in fulfilling it. They are there to paint Venice for us, the Venice of the magnificent young man. Bassanio embodies it also; but there are other calls on him, and he will be off to Belmont soon. So do Gratiano and Lorenzo; but they will be gone too. Solanio and Salarino will not fail us; they hoist this flag at the play's beginning and keep it bravely flying for as long as need be. When Salarino, for a beginning, addresses Antonio with

> There, where your argosies with portly sail,
> Like signiors and rich burghers on the flood,
> Or, as it were, the pageants of the sea,
> Do overpeer the petty traffickers,
> That curt'sy to them, do them reverence
> As they fly by them with their woven wings.

—there should be no skipping merriment in this.

They are argosies themselves, these magnificent young men, of high-flowing speech; pageants to overpeer the callow English ruffians, to whom they are here displayed. The talk passes from spices and silks into fine classical phrases; and with what elaborate, dignified dandyism it ends!

Enter Bassanio, Lorenzo and Gratiano.

Solanio. Here comes Bassanio, your most noble kinsman,
  Gratiano, and Lorenzo. Fare you well;
  We leave you now with better company.
Salarino. I would have stayed till I had made you merry,
  If worthier friends had not prevented me.
Antonio. Your worth is very dear in my regard.
  I take it, your own business calls on you,
  And you embrace the occasion to depart.
Salarino. Good-morrow, my good lords.
Bassanio. Good signiors both, when shall we laugh? Say, when?

---

[9] But Rosencrantz and Guildenstern, as Shakespeare wrote them, are not the mere puppets that the usual mangling of the text leaves them.

You grow exceeding strange: Must it be so?
Salarino. We'll make our leisures to attend on yours.

No apologetic gabbling here: but such a polish, polish as might have satisfied Mr. Turveydrop. Solanio—if one could distinguish between them—might cut the finer figure of the two. When the Masque is in question:

'Tis vile [he says], unless it may be quaintly ordered,
And better, in my mind, not undertook.

Salarino has a cultured young gentleman's turn for classical allusion. He ranges happily from two-headed Janus and Nestor to Venus' pigeons.

But it is, as we said, when Bassanio and Gratiano and Lorenzo with his Jessica have departed, that the use these two are to the play becomes plainest. They give us the first news of Antonio's losses, and hearsay, filtering through them, keeps the disaster conveniently vague. If we saw the blow fall on Antonio, the far more dramatic scene in which Shylock is thrown from depth to heights and from heights to depth as ill news and this good news strike upon him would be left at a discount. In this scene they are most useful (if they are not made mere targets for a star actor to shoot at). For here again is Venice, in the contrast between sordid Shylock and Tubal and our magnificent young gentlemen, superfine still of speech and manner, but not above a little Jew-baiting. They sustain that theme—and it must be sustained—till it can be fully and finally orchestrated in the trial-scene. It is a simple stagecraft which thus employs them, and their vacuity as characters inclines us to forget this, their very real utility. Forgetting it, Shakespeare's histrionic Venice is too often forgotten also.

THE CHARACTERS,
AND THE CRISIS OF THE ACTION

None of the minor characters does much more than illustrate the story; at best, they illuminate with a little lively detail their own passage through it. Not the Duke, nor Morocco, Aragon, Tubal, Lorenzo, Jessica, nor the Gobbos, nor Nerissa, had much being in Shakespeare's mind, we feel, apart from the scenes they played, and the use they were to him. It is as futile, that is to say, to discuss Jessica's excuses for gilding herself with ducats when she elopes as it is to work out her itinerary via Genoa to Belmont; we might as well start writing the life-story of Mistress Margery Gobbo.

Portia

Shakespeare can do little enough with Portia while she is still the slave of the caskets; incidentally, the actress must resist the temptation to try and do more. She has this picture of an enchanted princess to present, verse and prose to speak perfectly, and she had better be content with that. But we feel, nevertheless (and in this, very discreetly, she may at once encourage us), that here, pent up and primed for escape, is one of that eminent succession of candid and fearless souls: Rosaline, Helena, Beatrice, Rosalind—they embodied an ideal lodged for long in Shakespeare's imagination; he gave it expression whenever he could. Once he can set his Portia free to be herself, he quickly makes up for lost time. He has need to; for from the moment of that revealing

> You see me, Lord Bassanio, where I stand. . . .

not half the play's life is left her, and during a good part of this she must pose as the young doctor of Rome whose name is Balthasar. He does not very deliberately develop her character; he seems by now to know too much about her to need to do that. He reveals it to us mainly in little things, and lets us feel its whole happy virtue in the melody of her speech. This it is that casts its spell upon the strict court of Venice. The

> Shed thou no blood. . . .

is an effective trick. But

> The quality of mercy is not strained;
> It droppeth as the gentle rain from heaven
> Upon the place beneath. . . .

with its continuing beauty, gives the true Portia. To the very end she expands in her fine freedom, growing in authority and dignity, fresh touches of humor enlightening her, new traits of graciousness showing. She is a great lady in her perfect simplicity, in her ready tact (see how she keeps her guest Antonio free from the mock quarrel about the rings), and in her quite unconscious self-sufficiency (she jokes without embarrassment about taking the mythical Balthasar to her bed, but she snubs Gratiano the next minute for talking of cuckoldry, even as she snubbed Nerissa for a very mild indelicacy—she is fond of Nerissa, but no forward waiting-women for her!). Yet she is no more than a girl.

Here is an effect that we are always apt to miss in the acting of

Shakespeare today. It is not the actress's fault that she cannot be what her predecessor, the boy-Portia, was; and she brings us compensation for losses which should leave us—if she will mitigate the losses as far as she can—gainers on the whole. But the constant play made in the Comedies upon the contrast between womanly passion or wisdom and its very virginal enshrining gives a delicacy and humor to these figures of romance which the limited resources of the boy left vivid, which the ampler endowment of the woman too often obscures. This is no paradox, but the obvious result of a practical artistry making the most of its materials. Portia does not abide in this dichotomy as fully as, for instance, Rosalind and Viola do; but Shakespeare turns it to account with her in half a hundred little ways, and to blur the effect of them is to rob her of much distinction.

The very first line she speaks, the

By my troth, Nerissa, my little body is aweary of this great world.

is likely to come from the mature actress robbed of half its point. This will not matter so much. But couple that "little body" with her self-surrender to Bassanio as

an unlessoned girl, unschooled, unpractised;
Happy in this, she is not yet so old
But she may learn. . . .

and with the mischief that hides behind the formal courtesies of the welcome to Aragon and Morocco, with the innocence of the amazed

What no more!
Pay him six thousand and deface the bond. . . .

with the pretty sententiousness of her talk of herself, her

I never did repent of doing good,
Nor shall not now. . . .

followed by the artless

This comes too near the praising of myself. . . .

and the figure built up for us of the heiress and great lady of Belmont is seen to be a mere child, too, who lives remote in her enchanted world. Set beside this the Portia of resource and command, who sends Bassanio post haste to his friend, and beside that the schoolgirl laughing with Nerissa over the trick they are to play their new lords and masters. Know them all for one Portia, a wise and gallant spirit so virginally enshrined; and we see to what profit Shakespeare turned his disabilities. There is, in this play, a twofold artistry in the achievement.

Unlikelihood of plot is redeemed by veracity of character; while the artifice of the medium, the verse and its convention, and the stylized acting of boy as woman, re-reconciles us to the fantasy of the plot.

But a boy-Portia's advantage was chiefly manifest, of course, in the scene of the trial; and here in particular the actress of today must see that she lessens it no more than she need. The curious process of what we may call the "double negative," by which an Elizabethan audience first admitted a boy as a girl and then enjoyed the pretense that the girl was a boy, is obsolete for us; make-believe being the game, there was probably some pleasure just in this complication of it. This beside, there was the direct dramatic effect, which the boy made supremely well in his own person, of the wise young judge, the Daniel come to judgment. Shylock (and Shakespeare) plucks the allusion from the popular story of Susanna; but there may be some happy confusion, perhaps, with that other Daniel who was among ". . . the children of Israel, of the king's seede and of the Prince's: Springaldes without any blemish, but well-favoured, studious in all wisdome, skillful for knowledge, able to utter knowledge, and such as have livelinesse in them, that they might stand in the king's palace. . . ." For this is the very figure we should see. Here is the strict court of Venice, like enough to any law court, from East to West, from Shakespeare's time to now, in that it will seem to the stranger there very dry and discouraging, airless, lifeless. Age and incredulity preside; and if passion and life do enter, they must play upon muted strings. The fiercely passionate Shylock is anomaly enough in such surroundings. Then comes this youth, as brisk and businesslike as you please, and stands before the judges' bench, alert, athletic, modest, confident. He is life incarnate and destined to victory; and such a victory is the fitting climax to a fairy tale. So the Portia that will—as most Portias do—lapse into feminine softness and pitch the whole scene in the key of the speech on mercy, and that in a key of sentiment, damns the scene and herself and the speech, all three. This amazing youth has the ear of the court at once; but he'll only hold it by strict attention to business. Then, suddenly, out of this, comes the famous appeal, and catches us and the court unaware, catches us by the throat, enkindles us. In this lies the effect. Prepare for it, or make the beauty of it overbeautiful (all the more now, because it is famous and hackneyed) and it becomes a dose of soothing syrup.

This, be it further remembered, is not the scene's top note; conflict and crisis are to come. They are brought about simply and directly; the mechanical trick of the "No jot of blood" that is to resolve them asks nothing else. Shakespeare keeps the medium of the verse as simple; it flows on with hardly a broken line. The conflict is between Portia and Shylock. Bassanio's agony, Antonio's stoic resignation cannot be given great play; the artifice of the story will not even now sustain cross-currents of human passion. But the constraint of the business of a court accounts well enough for their quiescence (the actors need do nothing to discount it) and the few notes that are struck from them suffice. The action must sweep ahead and no chance be given us to question its likelihood. Even when all is over the Duke departs with not much more comment upon this amazing case than an invitation to the learned young doctor to come to dinner, and Antonio and his friends are as casual about it and almost as calm. There is tactful skill in this. Shylock has gone, that fairy tale is done with; the less we look back upon it, the sooner we come to fresh comedy again the better.

Throughout the scene a Portia must, of course, by no smallest sign betray to us—as well betray it to Bassanio—that she is other than she now seems. No difficulty here, as we said, for Shakespeare's Portia, or his audience either. There was no wondering as he faced the judges why they never saw this was a woman (since very obviously he now wasn't) nor why Bassanio did not know his wife a yard off. The liquid sentences of the Mercy speech were no betrayal, nor did the brusque aside of a young lawyer, intent upon his brief—

> Your wife would give you little thanks for that,
> If she were by to hear you make the offer.

—lose its quite casual humor. All this straightforwardness the modern actress must, as far as she can, restore.

Antonio, Gratiano and Others

In these early plays character does not as a rule outrun the requirements of the plot. Shakespeare is content enough with the decorative, the sententious, the rhetorical, in his casual Venetians, in Aragon and Morocco; with the conventional in Launcelot, who is the stage clown —the juggler with words, neat, agile, resourceful and occasionally familiar with the audience, as a clown and a juggler should be—under a thin disguise of character; with old Gobbo for a minute or two's incidental fun; with the pure utility of Tubal.

Antonio is flesh and blood. He is the passive figure of the story's demand; but Shakespeare refines this in the selflessness that can send Bassanio to Belmont and be happy in a friend's happiness, in the indifference to life that lets him oppose patience to his enemy's fury; and he makes him more convincingly this sort of man by making him just a little self-conscious too.

> In sooth, I know not why I am so sad. . . .

If he does not, it is not for want of thinking about it. He takes a sad pleasure in saying that he is

> a tainted wether of the flock,
> Meetest for death . . .

But there is a redeeming ironic humor in

> You cannot better be employed, Bassanio,
> Then to live still and write mine epitaph.

He is sufficiently set forth, and there is conveyed in him a better dignity than mere words give.[10]

Nerissa is echoing merriment; not much more.

Shakespeare may have had half a mind to make something a little out of the way of Gratiano. He starts him with a temperament and a witty speech; but by the play's end we have not had much more from him than the "infinite deal of nothing" of Bassanio's gibe, rattling stuff, bouncing the play along, but revealing no latent Gratiano. It all makes a good enough pattern of this sort of man, who will be a useful foil to Bassanio, and can be paired off for symmetry with Portia's foil, Nerissa; and the play needed no more. But there is enough of him, and enough talk about him, for one to feel that he missed by only a little the touch of magic that would have made something more of him and added him to the list of those that survive the lowering of the lights and the theater's emptying. There is a moment while he waits to take his share in Jessica's abduction, and sits reflecting:

> All things that are,
> Are with more spirit chased than enjoyed.
> How like a yonker or a prodigal,
> The scarfed bark puts from her native bay,
> Hugg'd and embraced by the strumpet wind!
> How like a prodigal doth she return;
> With over-weather'd ribs, and ragged sails,
> Torn, rent and beggared by the strumpet wind!

Harsh enough similes for such an occasion! Is this another side to the agreeable rattle? Does the man who exclaims

> Let me play the fool!
> With mirth and laughter let old wrinkles come. . . .

---

[10] It is worth remarking that the word "sad," as Shakespeare uses it, may mean rather solemn and serious than definitely miserable.

find life in fact rather bitter to his taste? But one must beware of reading subtleties into Shakespeare. If such a Gratiano was ever shadowed in his mind, he made no solid substance of him.

Bassanio we have spoken of; play the part straightforwardly and it will come right.

Shylock

There remains Shylock. He steps into the play, actual and individual from his first word on, and well might in his strength (we come to feel) have broken the pinchbeck of his origin to bits, had a later Shakespeare had the handling of him. As it is, his actuality is not weakened by the fantasy of the bond, as is Portia's by her caskets. For one thing, our credulity is not strained till the time comes for its maturing, and by then—if ever—the play and its acting will have captured us. For another, the law and its ways are normally so uncanny to a layman that the strict court of an exotic Venice might give even stranger judgments than this and only confirm us in our belief that once litigation begins almost anything may happen. Despite the borrowed story, this Shylock is essentially Shakespeare's own. But if he is not a puppet, neither is he a stalking-horse; he is no more a mere means to exemplifying the Semitic problem than is Othello to the raising of the color question. "I am a Jew." "Haply, for I am black. . . ." Here we have—and in Shylock's case far more acutely and completely—the *circumstances* of the dramatic conflict; but at the heart of it are men; and we may surmise, indeed, that from a maturer Shakespeare we should have had, as with Othello, much more of the man, and so rather less of the alien and his griefs. However that may be, he steps now into the play, individual and imaginatively full-grown, and the scene of his talk with Bassanio and Antonio is masterly exposition.

The dry taciturnity of his

Three thousand ducats; well?

(the lure of that thrice-echoed "Well"!) and the cold dissecting of the business in hand are made colder, drier yet by contrast with the happy sound of Portia's laughter dying in our ears as he begins to speak. And for what a helpless innocent Bassanio shows beside him; overanxious, touchy, overcivil! Shylock takes his time; and suddenly we see him peering, myopic, beneath his brows. Who can the newcomer be? And the quick brain answers beneath the question's cover: They must need the money badly if Antonio himself comes seeking me. Off goes Bassanio to greet his friend; and Shylock in a long aside can discharge his obligations to the plot.[11] These eleven lines are worth comment. In them is all the motive power for drama that the story, as Shakespeare found it, provides; and he throws this, with careless opulence, into a single aside. Then he returns to the upbuilding of *his* Shylock.

Note the next turn the scene takes. From the snuffling depreciation of his present store, for his own wonted fawning on these Christian clients, Shylock unexpectedly rises to the dignities of

> When Jacob grazed his uncle Laban's sheep . . .

And with this the larger issue opens out between Gentile and Jew, united and divided by the scripture they revere, and held from their business by this tale from it—of flocks and herds and the ancient East. Here is another Shylock; and Antonio may well stare, and answer back with some respect—though he recovers contempt for the alien creature quickly enough. But with what added force the accusation comes:

> Signior Antonio, many a time and oft
> In the Rialto you have rated me. . . .
> You called me misbeliever, cut-throat dog,
> And spit upon my Jewish gaberdine. . . .

The two Venetians see the Ghetto denizen again, and only hear the bondman's whine. But to us there is now all Jewry couched and threatening there, an ageless force behind it. They may make light of the money bond, but we shall not.

Shakespeare keeps character within the bounds of story with great tact; but such a character as this that has surged in his imagination asks more than such a story to feed on. Hence, partly at least, the new theme of Jessica and her flight, which will give Shylock another and more instant grudge to satisfy. It is developed with strict economy. Twenty-one lines are allowed to Jessica and Launcelot, another twenty or so to her lover and their plans; then, in a scene not sixty long, Shylock and his household are enshrined. As an example of dramatic thrift alone this is worth remark. The parting with Launcelot: he has a niggard liking for the fellow, is even hurt a little by his leaving, touched in pride, too, and shows it childishly.

> Thou shalt not gormandize
> As thou hast done with me. . . .

---

[11] This is one of the ever-recurring small strokes of stagecraft that are hardly appreciable apart from an Elizabethan stage. Shylock and Bassanio are to the front of the platform. Antonio, near the door, is by convention any convenient distance off; by impression, too, with no realistic scenery to destroy the impression. Shylock is left isolated, so isolated that the long aside has all the importance and the force of a soliloquy.

But he can at least pretend that he parts with him willingly and makes some profit by it. The parting with Jessica, which we of the audience know to be a parting indeed; that constant calling her by name, which tells us of the lonely man! He has looked to her for everything, has tasked her hard, no doubt; he is her jailer, yet he trusts her, and loves her in his extortionate way. Uneasy stranger that he is within these Venetian gates; the puritan, who, in a wastrel world, will abide by law and prophets! So full a picture of the man does the short scene give that it seems hardly possible we see no more of him than this between the making of the bond and the climacteric outbreak of passion upon Jessica's loss and the news of Antonio's ruin.[12]

References to him abound; Shylock can never be long out of our minds. But how deliberate is the thrift of opportunity we may judge by our being shown the first effect of the loss on him only through the ever-useful eyes of Salarino and Solanio. This is politic, however, from other points of view. Look where the scene in question falls, between Morocco's choice of his casket and Aragon's. Here or hereabouts some such scene must come, for the progress of the Antonio and Shylock story cannot be neglected. But conceive the effect of such a tragic outcry as Shylock's own,

> So strange, outrageous, and so variable . . .

—of such strong dramatic meat sandwiched between pleasant conventional rhetoric. How much of the credibility of the casket story would survive the association, with how much patience should we return to it? But Salarino and Solanio tone down tragedy to a good piece of gossip, as it becomes young men of the world to do. We avoid an emotional danger zone; and, for the moment at least, that other danger of an inconvenient sympathy with "the dog Jew." When Shylock's outbreak of anguish does come, the play is nearer to its climax, Bassanio's choice is about to free Portia's story from its unreality, and his savage certainty of revenge upon Antonio will now depress the sympathetic balance against him.

But, considering the story's bounds, what a full-statured figure we already have! Compare the conventional aside, the statement of the theme, in the earlier scene, the bald

---

[12] And so strange has this seemed to many a producer of the play and actor of Shylock, that we have been given scenes of pantomime in which Shylock comes back from Bassanio's supper to find Jessica flown. The solitary figure with a lantern, the unanswered rapping at the door, has become all but traditional. Irving did it, Coghlan had already done something of the sort, and—I fancy—Booth. An ingenious variation upon a theme by Shakespeare, that yet merely enfeebles the theme. The lengthier elaboration of a Shylock seen distracted at the discovery of his loss is, of course, even more inadmissible, since Shakespeare has deliberately avoided the situation.

I hate him for he is a Christian. . . .

with the deluge of molten passion which descends upon the devoted
Solanio and Salarino, obliterating their tart humor; compare the
theme, that is to say, with its development, mere story with character,
and measure in the comparison Shakespeare's growing dramatic power.

In tone and temper and method as well this scene breaks away from
all that has gone before. The very start in prose, the brisk

Now, what news on the Rialto?

even, perhaps, Solanio's apology for former

slips of prolixity or crossing the plain highway of talk . . .

seem to tell us that Shakespeare is now asserting the rights of his own
imagination, means, at any rate, to let this chief creature of it, his
Shylock, off the leash. And verily he does.

The scene's method repays study. No whirling storm of fury is asked
for; this is not the play's crisis, but preparation for it still. Shylock is
wrapped in resentful sorrow, telling over his wrong for the thousandth
time. Note the repetition of thought and phrase. And how much more
sinister this sight of him with the wound festering than if we had seen
the blow's instant fall! His mind turns to Antonio, and the thrice told

let him look to his bond.

is a rope of salvation for him; it knots up the speech in a dreadful
strength. Then, on a sudden, upon the good young Salarino's reasonable supposition that what a moneylender wants is his money back;
who on earth would take flesh instead?—

What's that good for?

—there flashes out the savagery stripped naked of

To bait fish withal: if it will feed nothing else, it will feed my revenge.

Now we have it; and one salutes such purity of hatred. There follows
the famous speech—no need to quote it—mounting in passionate logic,
from its

He hath disgraced me . . . and what's his reason? I am a Jew.

to the height of

If a Jew wrong a Christian, what is his humility? Revenge. If a Christian
wrong a Jew, what should his sufferance be by Christian example? Why,
revenge. The villainy you teach me I will execute, and it shall go hard
but I will better the instruction.

This is a Shylock born of the old story, but transformed, and here a theme of high tragedy, of the one seemingly never-ending tragedy of the world. It is the theme for a greater play than Shakespeare was yet to write. But if this one cannot be sustained on such a height, he has at least for the moment raised it there.

Solanio and Salarino are quite oblivious to the great moral issue opened out to them; though they depart a little sobered—this Jew seems a dangerous fellow. There follows the remarkable passage with Tubal; of gruesome comedy, the apocalyptic Shylock shrunk already to the man telling his ill-luck against his enemy's, weighing each in scales (love for his daughter, a memory of his dead wife thrown in!) as he is used to weigh the coin which is all these Christians have left him for his pride. It is technically a notable passage, in that it is without conflict or contrast, things generally necessary to dramatic dialogue; but the breaking of a rule will be an improvement, now and then, upon obedience to it. So Shakespeare, for a finish, lowers the scene from its crisis, from that confronting of Christian and Jew, of hate with hate, to this raucous assonance of these two of a kind and mind, standing cheek to cheek in common cause, the excellent Tubal fueling up revenge.

Such a finish, ousting all nobility, both shows us another facet of Shylock himself (solid figure enough now to be turned any way his maker will) and is, as we saw, a shadow against which the high romance of Bassanio's wooing will in a moment shine the more brightly. Sharp upon the heels of this, he comes again; but once more apocalyptic, law incarnate now.

Shylock. Gaoler, look to him; tell me not of mercy;
  This is the fool that lent out money gratis:
  Gaoler, look to him.
Antonio.   Hear me yet, good Shylock.
Shylock. I'll have my bond; speak not against my bond:
  I have sworn an oath that I will have my bond.

Verse and its dignity are needed for this scene; and note the recurring knell of the phrases:

      I'll have my bond; I will not hear thee speak:
      I'll have my bond, and therefore speak no more.
      I'll not be made a soft and dull-eyed fool,
      To shake the head, relent, and sigh, and yield
      To Christian intercessors. Follow not;
      I'll have no speaking: I will have my bond.

Here is a Shylock primed for the play's great scene; and Shakespeare's Shylock wrought ready for a catastrophe, which is a deeper one by far than the story yields. For not in the missing of his vengeance on Antonio will be this Shylock's tragedy, but in the betrayal of the faith on which he builds.

> I've sworn an oath that I will have my bond. . . .

How many times has the synagogue not heard it sworn?

> An oath, an oath. I have an oath in Heaven. . . .

He has made his covenant with an unshakable God:

> What judgment shall I dread, doing no wrong?

—and he is to find himself betrayed.

It is the apocalyptic Shylock that comes slowly into court, solitary and silent, to face and to outface the Duke and all the moral power of Venice.[13] When he does speak he answers the Duke as an equal, setting a sterner sanction against easy magnanimity—at other people's expense! One could complain that this first appeal for mercy discounts Portia's. To some extent it does; but the more famous speech escapes comparison by coming when the spell of the young doctor is freshly cast on us, and by its finer content and larger scope. Structurally, the Duke's speech is the more important, for it sets the lists, defines the issue and provokes that

> I have possessed your grace of what I purpose;
> And by our holy Sabbath have I sworn
> To have the due and forfeit of my bond. . . .

So confident is he that he is tempted to shift ground a little and let yet another Shylock peep—the least likable of all. He goes on

> You'll ask me, why I rather choose to have
> A weight of carrion flesh, than to receive
> Three thousand ducats: I'll not answer that,
> But say it is my humour. . . .

Legality gives license to the hard heart. Mark the progression. While the sufferer cried

> The villainy you teach me I will execute, and it shall go hard but I will better the instruction.

with the law on his side it is

---

[13] Upon the modern stage he usually has Tubal for a companion; one has even seen him seconded by a small crowd of sympathetic Jews. How any producer can bring himself so to discount the poignant sight of that drab, heroic figure, lonely amid the magnificence around, passes understanding!

> What judgment shall I dread, doing no wrong?

from which he passes, by an easy turn, to the mere moral anarchy of

> The pound of flesh, which I demand of him,
> Is dearly bought; 'tis mine, and I will have it. . . .

and in satanic heroism stands defiant:

> If you deny me, fie upon your law!
> There is no force in the decrees of Venice.
> I stand for judgment. Answer: shall I have it?

There is a dreadful silence. For who, dwelling unquestioningly under covenant of law, shall gainsay him?

It says much for the mental hypnosis which the make-believe of the theater can induce that this scene of the trial holds us so spellbound. Its poetry adds to the enchantment—let anyone try rewriting it in prose— and the exotic atmosphere helps. But how much more is due to the embroidering of character upon story so richly that the quality of the fabric comes to matter little! Shakespeare, at any rate, has us now upon the elemental heights of drama. He cannot keep us there. Portia must perform her conjuring trick; perhaps this is why he gives Shylock full scope before she arrives. But he brings us down with great skill, maneuvering character to the needs of the story, and turning story to character's account.

The coming of the young judge's clerk does not impress Shylock. How should it? Little Nerissa! He has won, what doubt of it? He can indulge then—why not?—the lodged hate and loathing he bears Antonio. The Duke is busy with Bellario's letter and the eyes of the court are off him. From avenger he degenerates to butcher. To be caught, lickerish-lipped, by Bassanio; and Gratiano's rough tongue serves him as but another whetstone for savagery! He turns surly at first sight of the wise young judge—what need of such a fine fellow and more fine talk?—and surlier still when it is talk of mercy. He stands there, he tells them yet again, asking no favors, giving none.

> My deeds upon my head! I crave the law,
> The penalty and forfeit of my bond.

Why does Shakespeare now delay the catastrophe by a hundred lines, and let Portia play cat-and-mouse with her victim? From the story's standpoint, of course, to keep the excitement a while longer. We guess there is a way out. We wonder what it can be; and yet, with that knife shining, Antonio's doom seems to come nearer and nearer. This is dramatic child's play, and excellent of its sort. But into it much finer stuff is woven. We are to have more than a trick brought off;

there must be a better victory; this faith in which Shylock abides must be broken. So first she leads him on. Infatuate, finding her all on his side, he finally and formally refuses the money—walks into the trap. Next she plays upon his fanatical trust in his bond, sets him searching in mean mockery for a charitable comma in it—had one escaped his cold eye—even as the Pharisees searched their code to convict Christ. Fold by fold, the prophetic dignity falls from him. While Antonio takes his selfless farewell of his friend, Shylock must stand clutching his bond and his knife, only contemptible in his triumph. She leads him on to a last slaveringly exultant cry: then the blow falls.

Note that the tables are very precisely turned on him.

> if thou tak'st more,
> Or less, than just a pound, be it so much
> As makes it light or heavy in the substance,
> Or the division of the twentieth part
> Of one poor scruple, nay, if the scale do turn
> But in the estimation of a hair . . .

is exact retaliation for Shylock's insistence upon the letter of his bond. Gratiano is there to mock him with his own words, and to sound, besides, a harsher note of retribution than Portia can; for the pendulum of sympathy now swings back a little—more than a little, we are apt to feel. But the true catastrophe is clear. Shylock stood for law and the letter of the law; and it seemed, in its kind, a noble thing to stand for, ennobling him. It betrays him, and in the man himself there is no virtue left.

> Is *that* the law?

he gasps helplessly. It is his only thought. The pride and power in which legality had wrapped him, by which he had outfaced them all, and held Venice herself to ransom, are gone. He stands stripped, once more the sordid Jew that they may spit upon, greedy for money, and hurriedly keen to profit by his shame.

> I take this offer then; pay the bond thrice,
> And let the Christian go

Here is Shakespeare's Shylock's fall, and not in the trick the law plays him.

He is given just a chance—would the story let him take it!—to regain tragic dignity. What is passing in his mind that prompts Portia's

> Why doth the Jew pause? Take thy forfeiture.[14]

---

[14] See Furness for an elaborate, illuminating and witty comment upon the situation.

No, nothing, it would seem, but the thought that he will be well out of the mess with his three thousand ducats safe.

Shakespeare has still to bring his theme full circle. He does it with doubled regard to character and story.

> Why, then the devil give him good of it!
> I'll stay no longer question.

If he were not made to stay, by every canon of theatrical justice Shylock would be let off too lightly; wherefore we find that the law has another hold on him. It is but a logical extending of retribution, which Gratiano is quick to reduce to its brutal absurdity. Here is Shylock with no more right to a cord with which to hang himself than had Antonio to a bandage for his wound. These quibbling ironies are for the layman among the few delights of law. Something of the villainy the Jew taught them the Christians will now execute; and Shylock, as helpless as Antonio was, takes on a victim's dignity in turn. He stays silent while his fate, and the varieties of official and unofficial mercy to be shown him, are canvassed.[15] He is allowed no comment upon his impoverishing for the benefit of "his son Lorenzo" or upon his forced apostasy. But could eloquence serve better than such a silence?

> *Portia.* Art thou contented, Jew? What dost thou say?
> *Shylock.* I am content.

With the three words of submission the swung pendulum of the drama comes to rest. And for the last of him we have only

> I pray you give me leave to go from hence;
> I am not well. Send the deed after me,
> And I will sign it.

Here is the unapproachable Shakespeare. "I am not well." It nears banality and achieves perfection in its simplicity. And what a completing of the picture of Shylock! His deep offense has been against human kindness; he had scorned compassion and prayed God himself in aid of his vengeance. So Shakespeare dismisses him upon an all but ridiculous appeal to our pity, such as an ailing child might make that had been naughty; and we should put the naughtiness aside. He passes

---

[15] It is hard to see why Antonio's taking the money to pass on to "the gentleman that lately stole his daughter" and providing that, for his half-pardon "he presently become a Christian," should be so reprobated by some critics. If we have less confidence today than had Antonio in the efficacy of baptism, have we none left in the rightfulness of reparation? Not much in its efficacy, perhaps. Antonio, one must insist, does not mean to keep any of the money for himself. One hopes he never lapsed into self-righteousness in recalling this. Nothing is said, however, about the original three thousand ducats!

out silently, leaving the gibing Gratiano the last word, and the play's
action sweeps on without pause. There can be no greater error than
to gerrymander Shylock a strenuously "effective exit"—and most Shy-
locks commit it. From the character's point of view the significant simplicity of that

I am not well.

is spoiled; and from the point of view of the play the technical skill
with which Shakespeare abstracts from his comedy this tragic and dominating figure and avoids anticlimax after is nullified.

THE RETURN TO COMEDY

The tragic interest is posted to oblivion cavalierly indeed. Seven
lines suffice, and the Duke's processional departure. The business of the
rings is then briskly dispatched, and made the brisker by the businesslike matter of the signing of the deed being tacked to it. Thence to
Belmont; and while Lorenzo and Jessica paint its moonlit beauty for
us, Balthasar and his clerk have time to change costume and tire their
heads again for Portia and Nerissa. They have evidently, as we saw,
none too much time; for Launcelot is allowed a last—and an incongru-
ously superfluous—piece of clowning. But the musicians can play
ahead for an extra minute or two if hooks and eyes refuse to fasten,
and no one will notice the delay. The last stretch of dialogue is lively;
a comic quartet coming after the consort of viols, and it asks for a like
virtuosity. The play ends, pleasantly and with formality, as a fairy tale
should. One may wonder that the last speech is left (against tradition)
to Gratiano; but one practical reason is plain. Portia and Bassanio,
Antonio, Lorenzo and Jessica must pace off the stage in their stately
Venetian way, while Gratiano's harmless ribaldry is tossed to the audience as an epilogue. Then he and Nerissa, now with less dignity than
ever to lose, skip quickly after.

Love's Wealth and the Judgement of
The Merchant of Venice

by John Russell Brown

Of all the comedies, *The Merchant of Venice* is the most completely informed by Shakespeare's ideal of love's wealth. Each of Portia's suitors has to choose one of three caskets and he who chooses the one which contains a portrait of Portia, wins her as his bride. Each casket is of a different metal and each bears a motto: one of gold reads "Who chooseth me shall gain what many men desire," one of silver reads "Who chooseth me shall get as much as he deserves," and one of lead reads "Who chooseth me must give and hazard all he hath." Morocco, the type of those who make their choice in love for the sake of what they will "gain," chooses gold and finds inside a skull—a reminder that death must cancel all such gain; Arragon, who presumes to take what "he deserves," finds a fool's head; Bassanio who is willing to "give and hazard," who does not mind the quality of the casket if he finds Portia within it, chooses lead and wins the bride of his choice. It could not be otherwise if love's true wealth, unlike commercial wealth, should be "in bounty" cherished, if "giving," not "gaining" or "getting," is essential to love. And so by these contrasts, clearly and formally, the wooing of Portia is related to Shakespeare's ideal.

As in *The Comedy of Errors* and *The Shrew*, this ideal is contrasted with a frankly commercial wealth, but here Shakespeare has broadened his theme. Previously commerce has been presented, in contrast to love, as concerned solely with possession and gain; now Shakespeare shows that it can involve personal relationships as well. Both Shylock and Antonio get their livelihood by commerce, but Antonio is ready to submit the rights of commerce to the claims of love; he lends freely to his friend Bassanio without security, although he has squandered previous loans and although it involves risking his own life by giving a bond to

"*Love's Wealth and the Judgement of* The Merchant of Venice." *From* Shakespeare and His Comedies *by John Russell Brown (London: Methuen & Co. Ltd., 1957), pp. 62–75. Reprinted, with the deletion of the original footnotes, with the permission of the publisher.*

Shylock for a pound of his flesh. This is to "give and hazard." In contrast, Shylock, the Jew, demands his rights; repeatedly he claims his due according to the bond, and sees no reason to relent:

> *What judgement shall I dread, doing no wrong?* . . .
> *The pound of flesh, which I demand of him,*
> *Is dearly bought; 'tis mine and I will have it.*
> *If you deny me, fie upon your law!*
> *There is no force in the decrees of Venice.*
> *I stand for judgement: answer; shall I have it?*
>
> (IV.i.89–103)

Shylock stands "for law" (IV.i.142): he disregards the plea for mercy because it has no "compulsion" and he will not provide a surgeon to stop Antonio's wounds because there is no stipulation to that effect in the bond. He is content to cry:

> *My deeds upon my head! I crave the law,*
> *The penalty and forfeit of my bond.*   (IV.i.206–7)

In Shylock's eyes, this is to "get what he deserves." Both he and Antonio may be judged by the mottoes on the caskets.

The contrast between these two is emphasized much earlier in the play in a discussion about usury. As Antonio enters to negotiate the bond, Shylock discovers his hatred in an aside:

> *I hate him for he is a Christian,*
> *But more for that in low simplicity*
> *He lends out money gratis and brings down*
> *The rate of usance here with us in Venice.* . . .   (I.iii.43–6)

Shylock lends only for what he can gain, Antonio for the sake of friendship; he makes this clear to Shylock:

> *If thou wilt lend this money, lend it not*
> *As to thy friends; for when did friendship take*
> *A breed for barren metal of his friend?*
> *But lend it rather to thine enemy,*
> *Who, if he break, thou mayst with better face*
> *Exact the penalty.*   (I.iii.133–8)

This issue is maintained throughout the play. When Antonio is in prison because he cannot repay the loan, Shylock taunts him with "This is the fool that lent out money gratis" (III.iii.2). Such generosity restricts the exercise of Shylock's rights and, as Antonio recognizes, is the main cause of his malice:

> *I oft deliver'd from his forfeitures*
> *Many that have at times made moan* **to me;**
> *Therefore he hates.*   (III.iii.22–4)

It is sometimes argued that Shylock's affairs are so far removed in kind from the affairs of the lovers at Belmont, that the play falls into two parts. But, in one way the play is very closely knit, for, besides contrasting Shylock with Antonio, the discussion about usury is yet another contrast between him and Portia and Bassanio. As we have seen from the sonnets and *Romeo and Juliet,* Shakespeare saw love as a kind of usury, and so in their marriage Bassanio and Portia put Nature's bounty to its proper "use." Shylock practises a usury for the sake of gain and is prepared to enforce his rights; the lovers practice their usury without compulsion, for the joy of giving:

> *That use is not forbidden usury*
> *Which happies those that pay the willing loan.*   (Sonnet vi)

As soon as Bassanio has chosen the right casket, being ready to "give and hazard all," Portia knows love's "increase":

> *O love,*
> *Be moderate; allay thy ecstasy;*
> *In measure rein thy joy; scant this* **excess.**
> *I feel too much thy blessing: make it less,*
> *For fear I surfeit.*   (III.ii.111–5)

Antonio has already used the word "excess" meaning "usury," and remembering Juliet's:

> *. . . my true love is* grown *to such* excess
> *I cannot* sum up *sum of half my* wealth *. . .*

the same sense seems to be required here. Bassanio's first reaction is to wonder at the beauty of the portrait which he finds inside the casket, then he finds a scroll ("The continent and summary of my *fortune*") which tells him to *"claim"* his lady "with a loving kiss"; at this point he uses yet another commercial image:

> *A gentle scroll. Fair lady, by your leave;*
> *I* come by note, *to* give *and to* receive.   '(III.ii.140–1)

To "come by note" meant to present one's bill or I.O.U.; Bassanio has "ventured" all and can now claim his "fortune." But as every bill in the commerce of love implies both giving and receiving, he is ready "to give *and* to receive"; these are the conditions of love's usury and so it is fitting that their "bargain" (III.ii.195) should be "confirm'd, sign'd ratified" (III.ii.149) with an interchange of kisses.

The comparison of the two usuries is part of a more general comparison of commerce and love which is likewise maintained throughout the play. From the beginning Bassanio's quest has been described in commercial terms; indeed, he might have equal claim with Antonio and Shylock for the title of "The Merchant of Venice." To Antonio he outlines his plans as a means of getting "clear of all the debts" he owes (I.i.134), trying, with little success, to present his intention of paying court to Portia as a good business proposition. Antonio tells him that all this is unnecessary, that such values are inappropriate to friendship, and thereupon Bassanio changes his tone, praising Portia in the "innocence" (I.i.145) of his love: she is indeed rich, and—

> . . . *she is fair* and, *fairer than that word,*
> *Of wondrous virtues. . . .*   (I.i.162–3)

He *"values"* her as Cato's daughter, renowned for constancy and virtue, and her "sunny locks" are the *"golden* fleece" for which Jason ventured. The comparison with the golden fleece is particularly significant, for the phrase was used of the fortunes for which merchants ventured; Drake, for example, was said to have returned from his voyage round the world bringing "his golden fleece." In Bassanio's description of Portia there is a curious, but, to those who trade in love, a natural, confusion of her wealth, beauty, and virtue; all these comprise her wealth in love. In Bassanio's eyes she has all perfections, and, amazed by them, he sees no obstacle to his fortune:

> *I have a mind presages me such* thrift,
> *That I should questionless be* fortunate!   (I.i.175–6)

When Bassanio has chosen the right casket, and comes "by note, to give and to receive," Portia responds in similarly commerical terms:

> *You see me, Lord Bassanio, where I stand,*
> *Such as I am: though for myself alone*
> *I would not be ambitious in my wish,*
> *To wish myself much better; yet, for you*
> *I would be trebled twenty times myself;*
> *A thousand times more fair, ten thousand times*
> *More rich . . .*   (III.ii.150–6)

Portia desires greater wealth only for Bassanio's sake:

> *That only to stand high in your* account,
> *I might in virtues, beauties, livings, friends,*
> Exceed account . . .   (III.ii.157–9)

She cannot possess enough of this kind of wealth to enable her to give as generously as she would wish:

> *. . . but the* full sum *of me*
> *Is sum of something, which, to* term in gross,
> *Is an unlesson'd girl . . .*   (III.ii.159–61)

Bassanio's willingness to give and hazard is answered by Portia's giving, and the contract of love is complete. So the willing, generous, and prosperous transactions of love's wealth are compared and contrasted with Shylock's wholly commercial transactions in which gain is the object, enforcement the method, and even human beings are merely things to be possessed.

Normally in Shakespeare's early narrative comedies, hero and heroine are betrothed at the end of the very last scene of the play where there is little time for the expression of sentiment; *The Merchant of Venice* is the major exception to this, presenting Portia's modest, eager, rich-hearted committal to Bassanio in the third act. In consequence, Shakespeare is not only able to show how love's wealth is risked, given, and multiplied, but also how it is possessed. At the end of Portia's speech of self-giving, she "commits" herself to Bassanio:

> *. . . to be directed,*
> *As from her lord, her governor, her king.*
> (III.ii.166–7)

All her wealth is made over as if it were a commercial possession:

> *Myself and what is mine to you and yours*
> *Is now* converted: *but now I was the lord*
> *Of this fair mansion, master of my servants,*
> *Queen o'er myself; and even now, but now,*
> *This house, these servants and this same myself*
> *Are yours, my lord: I give them with this ring. . . .*
> (III.ii.168–73)

Bassanio is told never to part with the ring, and in his confused joy, he can only swear that he will keep it for life. The story of Portia and Bassanio is by no means complete at this point; love is not like merchandise, it is not simply a question of possessor and possessed.

This is at once apparent: when news comes that Shylock is about to enforce the penalty to which his bond entitles him, Portia finds she has yet more to give; she is ready to forego wealth and delay her marriage rights, and she urges Bassanio to leave for Venice before nightfall. A line sums up her response:

> *Since you are* dear bought, *I will love you* dear.
> (III.ii.316)

Pope relegated this to the foot of the page in his edition on the grounds that its commercial attitude was unworthy of Shakespeare, but "dear"

is used in the double sense of "expensively" and "with great affection";
the line, in fact, expresses Portia's willingness to continue to give joyfully in love. In the commerce of love, giving is the secret of keeping as
well as of gaining.

Under this impulse, Portia herself goes to Venice and, disguised as
a lawyer, defeats Shylock's claims. For this service she refuses payment:

> *He is well paid that is well satisfied;*
> *And I, delivering you, am satisfied*
> *And therein do* account *myself well* paid:
> *My mind was never yet more* mercenary.   (IV.i.415–8)

Not recognizing Portia in the young lawyer, Antonio and Bassanio
cannot know how deeply he is satisfied, how "dearly" he has given;
they do not know that he has acted with love's bounty. Portia chooses
to bring this to their knowledge by the trick of asking Bassanio for
the ring she gave him at their betrothal. At first he refuses because of
his vow, but when he is left alone with Antonio, his love for this friend
persuades him to send the ring to the young lawyer. This twist in the
plot is resolved in the last act, and still further illustrates the kind of
possession which is appropriate for love's wealth.

The act begins with music, and talk of ancient loves and of the harmony of the spheres, but when Portia, Bassanio, and Antonio enter,
all harmony seems threatened by a quarrel over the ring of gold, the
symbol of possession. They now talk about unfaithfulness, adultery,
and cuckoldry. Bassanio's story is most unplausible and he is in a difficult position; as Portia protests with mock seriousness:

> *What man is there so much unreasonable,*
> *If you had pleased to have defended it*
> *With any terms of zeal, wanted the modesty*
> *To urge the thing held as a ceremony?* . . .
> *I'll die for't but some woman had the ring.*   (V.i.203–8)

Bassanio can only say that he was unable to refuse the one

> . . . *that did uphold the very life*
> *Of my dear friend.* . . .
> *I was beset with shame and courtesy;*
> *My honour would not let ingratitude*
> *So much besmear it.*   (V.i.214–9)

But when Antonio interjects that he is willing to "be bound again,"
with his "soul upon the forfeit," that Bassanio will "never more break
faith advisedly" (V.i.251–3), Portia returns the ring, and perplexity is
soon resolved. And Bassanio is soon pardoned, for he has erred only
through generosity to his friend. The whole episode is a light-hearted

reminder that Portia has saved Antonio's life, and that the claim of generosity must always rank as high as that of possession.

The bawdy talk, which the misunderstandings provoke, also serves an important purpose; hitherto Bassanio and Portia have conducted their courtship and love in unsensual terms, almost as if the body was always a quietly acquiescing follower of the mind and spirit, but the manner in which they weather the disagreement about the ring shows that their love is appropriate to the world as well as to Belmont, the "beautiful mountain" of a fairy-tale. The wealth of love, although it exists in the free giving of both parties to the contract and is possessed by neither one of them, has yet to be kept safe and guarded: so the blunt, unromantic Gratiano who has been as merrily fooled by Nerissa as Bassanio has been by Portia, finishes the play:

> *Well, while I live I'll fear no other thing*
> *So sore as keeping safe Nerissa's ring.* (V.i.306–7)

After the ring episode, we know that Bassanio and Portia will be equally wise. If *The Merchant of Venice* is seen as a play about Shakespeare's ideal of love's wealth, this last act is a fitting sequel to the discord of the trial scene where love and generosity confront hatred and possessiveness; it suggests the way in which love's wealth may be enjoyed continually.

The central theme of love's wealth is amplified in many other details which may seem irrelevant on casual inquiry. So Jessica's story has its contribution; she escapes with Lorenzo from behind the locked doors of Shylock's house, squanders the Venetian wealth she has stolen in joyful celebration, and then finds peace and happiness with her *"unthrift* love" (V.i.16) in the garden of Belmont. If her reckless prodigality is a fault, it is a generous one and an understandable excess after the restriction of her father's precept of

> *Fast bind, fast find;*
> *A proverb never stale in* thrifty *mind.* (II.v.54–5)

She has her due place at Belmont. And Launcelot Gobbo earns his place there by joining Bassanio's household; Shylock may have good reason for calling him an *"unthrifty* knave" (I.iii.177) but we also recognize Launcelot's good sense in counting it a fine fortune

> *To leave a* rich *Jew's service, to become*
> *The follower of so* poor *a gentleman.* (II.ii.156–7)

The ideal of love's wealth which relates and contrasts Shylock and Antonio, and Shylock and Portia and Bassanio, also informs the contrasts and relationships between the subsidiary narrative plots; in the final scene the easily responsive love of Jessica and Lorenzo, the bolder

love of Gratiano and Nerissa, and Launcelot's unseeing pleasure in his
master's good fortune, all contribute to the judgement on life which
is implicit in the play as a whole.

The reservations which must be made before Jessica, Gratiano, and
Launcelot fit into the general pattern illustrate an important quality
of the play. Shakespeare has not simply contrived a contrast of black
and white, a measured interplay of abstract figures with every detail
fitting neatly into a predetermined pattern; the lovers are not all para-
gons and Shylock's cry for revenge is not without a "kind of wild justice." Judged against Shakespeare's ideal of love's wealth we cannot
doubt on which side our sympathies should rest, but such final harmony is only established after we have judged, as in life, between mixed
motives and imperfect responses. Even when the central theme has
been recognized, *The Merchant of Venice* is not an "easy" play; it
presents an action to which we must respond as to a golden ideal, and
also as to a human action.

We have already noticed Shakespeare's achievement of this double
purpose in dialogue; for example, when Portia gives herself to Bassanio
Shakespeare has not provided a well-rounded expression of generosity
in love for her to utter; her speech also embodies modesty, eagerness,
and a gathering confidence, feelings that in a human context must
attend such generosity. Action and dialogue are allied to the same end;
so Shakespeare presented Bassanio's ill-judged attempt to justify his
venture in commercial terms and followed that by his confused description of Portia's wealth, at first formal, then quickening, glowing, almost
boasting, and, finally, blindly confident. Such technique does not simply present a theoretical ideal of love's adventurer, but a human being,
fearful and eager, inspired and embarrassed as he realizes the possibili-
ties of love's wealth. In human terms his is a difficult role, for he must
feel the confusion of one who asks:

> . . . *how do I hold thee but by thy* granting?
> *And for that riches where is my deserving?*   (Sonnet lxxvii)

For the role of Bassanio the "humanizing" of action and dialogue has
been so thorough that its ideal implications are in some danger of
being obscured. Some critics have discounted the embarrassment of
love's largess and, because of his round-about approach to Antonio,
have called Bassanio a heartless "fortune-hunter"—and in doing so they
have failed to see the balance and judgement of the play as a whole.

Shylock is in greatest danger of causing such misinterpretation. This
is truly surprising, for in order to bring generosity and possessiveness
into intense conflict Shakespeare has made him perpetrate the out-
rageous deeds of some fantastic villain whom we might expect to see
punished without compunction. Moreover Shylock is a Jew and there-

fore, for an Elizabethan audience, one of an exotic, fabulous race to whom cunning, malice, and cruelty were natural satisfactions; Jews lived obscurely in Shakespeare's London, but in literature and popular imagination they were monstrous bogeys from strange, far-off places and times, fit only to be reviled or mocked. Shakespeare exploited both Shylock's irrational, or devilish, motivation and the outrage of his action, but he has presented him in such a way that an audience can find itself implicated in his inhuman demands. Shakespeare seems to have done everything in his power to encourage this reaction. Our revulsion from Shylock's hatred and cruelty is mitigated by the way in which his opponents goad and taunt him; we might suppose that he was driven to excessive hatred only through their persecution. Shakespeare also arranged that he should voice his grievances and plead his case in the play's most obviously lively and impassioned dialogue. This treatment is so successful that when Shylock tries to justify his murderous purpose, some critics have believed that he is making a grand, though tortured, plea for human tolerance. But to go to such lengths of sympathy for Shylock is to neglect the contrasts and comparisons implicit in the play as a whole; we must judge his actions against a purposefully contrasted generosity in love as portrayed by Antonio, Portia, Bassanio, and others. Indeed we may guess that it was in order to make this contrast lively and poignant that Shakespeare has laboured to implicate us in Shylock's hatred, frustration, and pain.

The outcome of the comparison cannot be long in question for judged by Shakespeare's ideal of love's wealth as expressed here and in other comedies, the sonnets and *Romeo and Juliet,* we cannot doubt that Shylock must be condemned. However lively Shylock's dialogue may be, however plausibly and passionately he presents his case, however cruelly the lovers treat him, he must still be defeated, because he is an enemy to love's wealth and its free, joyful, and continual giving; in opposition to this he has "contrived against the very life" (IV.i.360) of Antonio, the "fool that lent out money gratis."

But this judgement cannot be made lightly; the mirror that Shakespeare held up to nature was unsparing in its truth, and, by presenting his ideal in human terms, he has shown that those who oppose the fortunes of lovers are apt to get more than justice as punishment at their hands. It is Shylock's fate to bring out the worst in those he tries to harm: the "good Antonio" shows unfeeling contempt towards him, the light-hearted Salerio and Solanio become wantonly malicious when they meet him, and Portia, once she has turned the trial against him, wounds him still further with sarcastic humour. The trial scene shows that the pursuit of love's wealth does not necessarily bring with it a universal charity, a love which reaches even to one's enemies. The balance is fairly kept, for Antonio and the Duke magnanimously spare

Shylock's life and this is thrown into relief by the irresponsible malice of Gratiano.

Shakespeare does not enforce a moral in this play—his judgement is implicit only—but as the action ends in laughter and affection at Belmont we know that each couple, in their own way, have found love's wealth. We know too that their happiness is not all that we would wish; as they make free with Shylock's commercial wealth, we remember that they lacked the full measure of charity towards one who, through his hatred and possessiveness, had got his choice of that which he deserved. *The Merchant of Venice* presents in human and dramatic terms Shakespeare's ideal of love's wealth, its abundant and sometimes embarrassing riches; it shows how this wealth is gained and possessed by giving freely and joyfully; it shows also how destructive the opposing possessiveness can become, and how it can cause those who traffic in love to fight blindly for their existence.

Because such judgements are not made explicit in the play, we, as an audience in the theatre, may never become consciously aware of them; we would almost certainly fail in our response if, during performance, our whole attention was given to recognizing and elucidating such judgements. But, consciously or unconsciously, they were in Shakespeare's mind as he wrote the play and helped to control its shape, its contrasts, relationships and final resolution, and to direct and colour the detail of its dialogue; and it therefore follows that as we respond to the action and dialogue on the stage, as we follow with spontaneous interest and delight, these judgements will, consciously or unconsciously, impress themselves on our minds; they are the pattern of the dance that we are appreciating and in which, imaginatively, we participate. To understand that dance, to hold it more fully in our memory, we must also learn to appreciate its pattern; to understand the full beauty and truth of Shakespeare's comedy we must become conscious of the ideals and implicit judgements that inform it.

The Ideal Production

by G. Wilson Knight

The meaning of *The Merchant of Venice* is never sufficiently brought
out. We must take the play seriously. Its deeper significances do not,
it is true, correspond at every point with a surface realism as they do in
Macbeth. But for this very reason we must take care to bring the
inherent meaning out as harmoniously and as naturally, yet powerfully, as we can.

This play presents two contrasted worlds: Venice and Belmont. The
one is a world of business competition, usury, melancholy, and tragic
sea-disaster; the other, a spelled land of riches, music, and romance.
This I show in *The Shakespearian Tempest,* pp. 127–41. I know many
of our Venetian scenes are comparatively jovial: but Gratiano is
scarcely a pleasant man. Venice has romantic associations: but here it
is darkly toned. The supposedly pleasant people are not all they might
be. Antonio is cruel to Shylock, Bassanio a spendthrift, Gratiano vulgar,
and honesty certainly not the strongest point of Lorenzo and Jessica.
Shylock towers over the rest, grand, it is true, but scarcely amiable.
Observe that the tragedy depends on sea-wreck, tempests, and such like:
Shakespeare's usual tragedy associations. But at Belmont all this is
changed. All the people become noble as soon as they arrive there:
Bassanio is the loyal friend, Lorenzo the perfect lover, Gratiano is,
comparatively, subdued. The name Belmont suggests a height over-
looking the water-logged world of Venetian rivalry and pettiness. At
Belmont we have music continually: at Venice, none. The projected
Masque we may observe does not, as far as our persons are concerned,
come off after all (II,vi,64); but it serves for Shylock's significant lines
about the "vile squealing of the wry-neck'd fife," which might be com-
pared with his even less pretty "bagpipe" reference later. Certainly,
Venice is not here a place of romantic music. Belmont is. And the
Belmont world is dominated by Portia; expressly Christian, as against
Shylock, her only rival in dramatic importance; and of infinite wealth

---

"The Ideal Production" (Editor's title). From Principles of Shakespearian Production *by G. Wilson Knight (London: Faber and Faber, Ltd., 1936), pp. 135–40. Reprinted by permission of the publisher.*

as against the penurious Bassiano and thieving Lorenzo. Everyone in Venice is in money difficulties of some sort, even the rich ones. Antonio's fortune is all at sea. Shylock has to borrow from Tubal, and later loses a great part of his wealth with his daughter, and bemoans his lost ducats in the street. But Portia is infinitely rich. Her riches hold, dramatically, an almost spiritual quality.

Our permanent set must help to mark out these contrasted worlds. I suggest dividing the stage into two levels, the rise making a straight diagonal from up L to down R. The higher level is thus mainly on stage right. Half-way along this diagonal steps can be used to lead from one level to the other. Venetian scenes will concentrate on the lower, Belmont on the higher, level. I do not mean that no Venetian in Venice should ascend the higher: merely that the Venetian action should always focus on the lower with a force proportional to the particular significance. Certainly in the Belmont scenes the lower space must never be quite empty, which would tend to rob the figures above of any dignity their raised position gives them: a point we have already discussed. We can arrange a background that gives a wide and variable range of tones according to the lights: this will help. For the casket scenes the suitors enter down R or down L and ascend the steps ceremoniously. Nothing must seem too rigid, however. Portia, standing aside during Bassanio's meditations, would probably come down L on the lower level; and later meet him as he descends the steps, an action which suits the submissive femininity of her speech, and his victorious choice.

The three caskets will be large and solid-looking, and must be allowed to dominate. They are symbolically central to the play's action. At the heart of this play is the idea of riches: false and true wealth. Jesus' parables are suggested. Venice is lost in the varied complexities of the false. Portia possesses the true. Not only is love and beauty continually in Shakespeare metaphorically a matter of riches, but Portia is vitally associated with Christianity, and is, moreover, an heiress with an infinite bank-balance. In this play of greed her serene disregard of exact sums has something supernal about it:

> *Portia.* What sum owes he the Jews?
> *Bassanio.* For me three thousand ducats.
> *Portia.*   What, no more?
>   Pay him six thousand, and deface the bond;
>   Double six thousand, and then treble that . . .

He shall have gold "to pay the petty debt twenty times over." We must note further that Portia's office in the play is to demonstrate the futility, as a final resort, of business and legal exactitudes. The action drives home the truth that money is only an aspect of life, and that life itself must come before money and the laws of money.[1] The contrast is exquisitely pointed by the situation of a man giving a pound of flesh as security. Everyone wants to save his life, but there seems no loophole. His life is now subject to laws made only for money. Observe how Portia deals with the absurd situation. She dispels the clouding precisions and intellectualities of the law court by a serene common-sense. This is something very like the common-sense of Jesus. Her Mercy speech exactly reflects His teaching. Moreover, the white beam of her intuition shows, as genius has a way of showing, as Jesus' teaching so often shows, that the academic intelligence is itself vulnerable at every point by its own weapons. Shylock's worst danger is to be allowed the rights he fights for:

> The words expressly are "a pound of flesh":
> Take then thy bond; take thou thy pound of flesh;
> But, in the cutting it, if thou dost shed
> One drop of Christian blood . . .

This is what comes of not distinguishing between the counters of finance and the bread and wine, the silver flesh and golden blood, of life itself. The serene wisdom of life works always by refusing validity to false abstractions. You can cut money into bits, but not life; there any piece involves the whole. Such are the lines of Portia's reasoning; it is fundamentally a poetic and holistic reasoning. As soon as you begin to think in such poetic and holistic terms there are always certain supposed exactitudes that lose all meaning: so next Portia supports her first argument by insisting that poor Shylock shall take exactly a pound of flesh, neither less nor more by the weight of a hair. His whole position crumbles.

Clearly, then, the caskets, gold, silver and lead, containing respectively death, folly and infinite love and wealth, must be solid and dominating. This play is not so silly as many a modern critic would have it and many a modern production makes it.

So Venice and Belmont alternate. The play works up to the climax of the Trial Scene, where the protagonists of the two worlds, Portia and Shylock, meet for the first time. Portia descends from Belmont almost as a divine being:[2] her office is, anyway, that of a *dea ex machina*. I would have the court sitting on the high level R, some using the level itself for a seat. The Duke's chair will be half-way along. Bassanio and Antonio are down R; Shylock moves between up L, L, and C. Some

---

[1] I acknowledge a debt in my thinking around this point to Mr Max Plowman's most illuminating note, "Money and the Merchant," *The Adelphi*, Sept. 1931.

[2] Portia at Belmont is, to Morocco, a "shrine" and a "mortal breathing saint." The arrival of her wooers will stress this suggestion. They will face her on the steps, themselves standing below, as pilgrims before a divine sanctuary.

spectators can edge in down L and Gratiano stand L between them and Shylock, coming forward for his big speeches.

Portia enters down R, circles up-stage to the steps, and ascends the higher level, standing beside the Duke. Her doctor's gown is better neither black nor red. Her doctorate is one of serene Christian wisdom and feminine intuition. She never gained it at Padua. Let her therefore wear a correctly cut doctor-of-laws gown of spotless white.[3] She is high and central dominating the whole court. The light should be intensified on her white gown and golden hair just showing under her cap as she speaks her Mercy speech. But, as the situation ripens, she descends: observe how this movement uses our levels to capture the essence of her arrival in Venice to render assistance, her *descent* from the happier world of her home. She comes nearly, but not quite, down the steps at: "I pray you, let me look upon the bond." Shylock gives it her. She warns him: "Shylock, there's thrice thy money offered thee." She is kind, is meeting these people on their own terms, descending to their level. But Shylock will have none of it. She tries again. He returns to his corner, talking to Tubal, adamant. Portia, on the steps, begins to prepare judgment. She addresses Antonio, asks for balances and a surgeon. Antonio says his farewell. Now, swaying slightly, she pronounces judgment, the speed gathers as the whirl of her repetition gains force, the whirl of a lasso:

> The court awards it and the law doth give it,

and

> The law allows it and the court awards it.

Shylock, in ecstasy of hatred, cries "A sentence! Come, prepare!" Unleashed, he springs down-stage. Bassanio shields Antonio. The Duke stands. The crowds murmur. But at this instant Portia takes the last step down to the lower level and cuts off Shylock's attack with a raised hand, "Tarry a little." There is silence. In a quiet voice she continues:

> . . . there is something else.
> This bond doth give thee here no jot of blood . . .

The terrible judgment of a fathomless simplicity and divine common-sense.

It is, of course, an amazing scene, and its tremendous dramatic impact derives from the clash of the two dominating forces in the play, Shylock and Portia, and all that they stand for. Our set of two levels with Portia's descent will assist; so will her white gown, and her sig-

---

[3] Something suitable must be devised for Nerissa, who enters with Portia. The gown I advocate for Portia reflects exactly that blend of realism and symbolic meaning which I regard as the essential quality of Shakespearian drama.

nificant barring of Shylock's attack at the crucial moment, which must be given expressive action. We must work always from the profound issues implicit in the dramatic thrill if it is to have full power. Portia's standing on the same steps where previously we have seen her meet her suitors, with the caskets behind, priestess of the knowledge of true and false wealth, clearly helps this scene. We are aware of her bringing her own world and all it symbolizes into the new context.

For the rest of the scene do not be afraid of an anti-climax. Portia must be firm and not too pitiful. Shylock's exit, C to down L through the crowd, can be as pathetic as you will, but not too long delayed. The play shows a Christian, romantic, and expressly feminine Portia against a down-trodden, vengeful, racially grand, usurious Jew. I do not claim that all the difficulties inherent in this opposition are finally settled in our play: but I do claim that this dramatic opposition is a profound one. You must not suppose that since Portia has all our sympathy Shylock can have none: poetic drama can be paradoxical. Portia stands serene in white purity, symbol of Christian romance. But Shylock, saying he is ill, picks up his cloak and goes out robed in purple: the purple of tragedy. Two tremendous imaginative issues conflict: the romantic dream and tragic realism. Later Shakespeare is to reconcile them. Here the opposition must be stark: neither must be watered down.

The last scene at Belmont acts itself easily: but I object to so unfortunate a back-cloth as one with waves painted on it, for obvious reasons. Our set here might for the first time dispose of the change. Our set here might for the first time dispose of the change in level. The action's dualism may not have been perfectly unified: but you certainly are not supposed now to be worrying about it. Or again, you might keep it, and get highly significant comedy out of the lovers chasing each other—as they usually do—about from one level to the other. On second thoughts, I think this best. It would have meaning. Lorenzo and Jessica would be comfortably placed on the steps at the beginning.

Frank Kermode: Some Themes in *The Merchant of Venice*

We are not likely, whether or not we share his high opinion of Shakespeare as a comic writer, to fall into Johnson's error when he dismissed the reiteration of the word "gentle" in this play as only another example of Shakespeare's weakness for this "fatal Cleopatra," the pun. "Gentleness" in this play means civility in its old full sense, nature improved; but it also means "Gentile," in the sense of Christian, which amounts, in a way, to the same thing. Here are some of the passages in which it occurs:

> Hie thee, gentle Jew.
> The Hebrew will turn Christian: he grows kind.   (l.iii.178)

> If e'er the Jew her father come to heaven,
> It will be for his gentle daughter's sake.   (II.iv.34)
> (Jessica is also called "gentle" in l. 19)

> Now, by my hood, a Gentile [gentle] and no Jew.   (II.vi.51)
> . . . to leave a rich Jew's service and become
> The follower of so poor a gentleman.   (II.ii.756)

The Duke urges Shylock to be merciful; asking him not only to

> loose the forfeiture,
> But, touch'd with human gentleness and love,
> Forgive a moiety of the principal. . . .
> We all expect a gentle answer, Jew.   (IV.i.24)

Other "gentle" objects are Antonio's ships, and Portia, many times over; and Portia speaks of mercy as a "gentle rain."

There is a straightforward contrast between gentleness, the "mind of love," and its opposite, for which Shylock stands. He lends money at interest, which is not only unchristian, but an obvious misdirection of love; Antonio ventures with his ships, trusts his wealth to the hand

---

"*Some Themes in* The Merchant of Venice" (*Editor's title*) *by Frank Kermode. From* Stratford-upon-Avon Studies 3: Early Shakespeare, *ed. John Russell Brown and Bernard Harris (London: Edward Arnold (Publishers) Ltd., 1961), pp. 221–24. Reprinted by permission of the publisher.*

of God (and so they are "gentle" ships). It is true that a Jew hath eyes
etc.; this does not reduce the difference between man and man, when
one is gentle and the other not. To make all this clear, Shakespeare
twice inserts the kind of passage he later learned to do without; the
kind which tells the audience how to interpret the action. It is normal
to cut these scenes in acting texts, but only because these plays are
so grossly misunderstood. The first such is the debate on Genesis,
xxxi.37 ff. (Jacob's device to produce ringstraked, speckled and spotted
lambs) which occurs when Antonio first asks for the loan (I.iii.66 ff).
The correct interpretation of this passage, as given by Christian commentators on Genesis (see A. Williams, *The Common Expositor,* 1950),
is that Jacob was making a venture ("A thing not in his power to bring
to pass,/But sway'd and fashion'd by the hand of heaven"; compare
Faerie Queene, V. iv). But Shylock sees no difference between the
breeding of metal and the breeding of sheep—a constant charge against
usurers (ese J. R. Brown's note on the passage in his Arden edition,
where he rightly points out that this was commonplace). Later, in II.
viii, we have a pair of almost Spenserian *exampla* to make this point
clear. First Solanio describes Shylock's grief at the loss of daughter and
ducats; he cannot distinguish properly between them, or lament the
one more than the other. Then Solario describes the parting of Antonio
and Bassanio; Antonio urges Bassanio not even to consider money;
the loss of Bassanio is serious, but he urges him to be merry and not
to think of Shylock's bond. When love is measured out, confused by
the "spirit of calculation" (R. B. Heilman's phrase in his discussion
of the errors of Lear),[1] the result is moral chaos.

Bassanio's visit to Belmont is frankly presented as a venture, like
Jason's for the Golden Fleece; and the theme of gentle venturing is
deepened in the scenes of the choice of caskets. The breeding metals,
gold and silver, are to be rejected; the good lead requires that the
chooser should "give and hazard all he hath." Morocco (II.vii) supposes
that Portia cannot be got by any casket save the golden one, tacitly con-
fusing her living worth with that of gold, the value of gentleness with
that of the best breeding metal. Arragon (II.ix—the intervening scene
contains the lamentation of Shylock over his daughter-ducats) rejects
gold out of pride only, ironically giving the right reasons for despising
the choice of the "many," that they are swayed not by Truth but by
Opinion, a mere false appearance of Truth, not Truth itself. (In this
sense the Jews are enslaved to Opinion.) He chooses silver because he
"assumes desert," another matter from trusting to the hand of God;
and his reward is "a shadow's bliss." After another scene in which
Shylock rejoices over Antonio's losses and again laments Jessica's treach-

---

[1] *"The Unity of King Lear"* in *Critiques & Essays in Criticism 1920–1948,* ed. R. W.
Stallman (1949), pp. 154–161; and see Heilman, *This Great Stage* (1948) .

ery, there follows (III.ii) the central scene of choice, in which Bassanio comes to "hazard" (2) and "venture" (10) for Portia. The point of the little song is certainly that in matters of love the eye is a treacherous agent, and can mistake substance for shadow. Bassanio, rejecting the barren metals which appear to breed, avoids the curse of barrenness on himself (for that is the punishment of failure); and he finds in the leaden casket Portia's true image. The scroll speaks of the "fortune" which has fallen to him (133). Portia, in her happiness, speaks of Bassanio's prize as not rich enough, deploring the poorness of her "full sum" (158); and Gratiano speaks of the forthcoming marriage as the solemnization of "the bargain of your faith." Bassanio the merchant has "won the fleece"; but at the same moment Antonio has lost his (243–4). Bassanio is "dear bought," as Portia says; but Antonio will not have him return for any reason save love: "if your love do not persuade you to come, let not my letter" (322).

At this point the conflict between gentleness (Antonio's laying down his life for his friend) and a harsh ungentle legalism becomes the main burden of the plot. Shylock demands his bond; this is just, like Angelo's strict application of the law against fornication in the hard case of Claudio. It is, in a way, characteristic of Shakespeare's inspired luck with his themes that Shylock in the old stories will take flesh for money. There is no substantial difference: he lacks the power to distinguish gold, goat's flesh, man's flesh, and thinks of Antonio's body as carrion. The difference between this and a "gentle" attitude reflects a greater difference:

> *Duke.* How shalt thou hope for mercy, rendering none?
> *Shylock.* What judgement shall I dread, doing no wrong?   (IV.i.87)

There is no need to sentimentalize this; as Shakespeare is careful to show in *Measure for Measure* the arguments for justice are strong, and in the course of Christian doctrine it is necessarily satisfied before mercy operates. Mercilla has her blunted sword, but also the sharp one for punishment, and she "could it sternly draw" (*Faerie Queene*, V.ix.30). Shylock has legally bought his pound of flesh; if he does not get it "there is no force in the decrees of Venice" (IV.i.102). But as heavenly mercy is never deserved, it is an adornment of human authority to exercise it with the same grace:

> . . . earthly power doth then show likest God's
> When mercy seasons justice. Therefore, Jew,
> Though justice be thy plea, consider this,
> That, in the course of justice, none of us
> Should see salvation.   (196)

But this plea does not work on the stony unregenerate heart; Shylock persists in the demand for justice, and gets it. Like any other human being, he must lose all by such a demand. In offering to meet the demands of strict justice (in accordance with the Old Law) Antonio will pay in blood the price of his friend's happiness; and it cannot be extravagant to argue that he is here a type of the divine Redeemer, as Shylock is of the unredeemed.

Shakespeare's last act, another "thematic" appendix to the dramatic action, is motivated by the device of the rings. It begins with a most remarkable passage, Lorenzo's famous "praise of music." In this are treated "topics" which, as James Hutton shows in an extremely important study,[2] are all evidently the regular parts of a coherent and familiar theme—so familiar indeed, that Shakespeare permits himself to treat it "in a kind of shorthand." The implications of this "theme" are vast; but behind it lies the notion, very explicit in Milton's "Ode at a Solemn Musick," of the universal harmony impaired by sin and restored by the Redemption. The lovers, in the restored harmony of Belmont, have a debt to Antonio:

> You should in all sense be much bound to him,
> For, as I hear, he was much bound for you.   (V.i.136)

In such an atmosphere the amorous sufferings of Troilus, Thisbe, Dido and Medea are only shadows of possible disaster, like the mechanicals' play in *A Midsummer Night's Dream*; Antonio on his arrival is allowed, by the *contretemps* of the ring-plot, to affirm once more the nature of his love, standing guarantor for Bassanio in perpetuity, "my soul upon the forfeit" (V.i.252). *The Merchant of Venice*, then, is "about" judgment, redemption and mercy; the supersession in human history of the grim four thousand years of unalleviated justice by the era of love and mercy. It begins with usury and corrupt love; it ends with harmony and perfect love. And all the time it tells its audience that this is its subject; only by a determined effort to avoid the obvious can one mistake the theme of *The Merchant of Venice*.

[2] "Some English Poems in Praise of Music," *English Miscellany* II (1951), 1–63.

A. D. Moody: An Ironic Comedy

The established view of *The Merchant of Venice* goes something like this:

The Merchant of Venice, then, is "about" judgement, redemption and mercy; the supersession in human history of the grim four thousand

"An Ironic Comedy." From Shakespeare: The Merchant of Venice *by A. D. Moody (London: Edward Arnold (Publishers) Ltd., 1964), pp. 9–15, 53–56. Reprinted by permission of the author and the publisher.*

years of unalleviated justice by the era of love and mercy. It begins with usury and corrupt love; it ends with harmony and perfect love.[1]

Professor Frank Kermode, whose formulation this is, supports it with the assertion that "only by a determined effort to avoid the obvious" can one fail to see that that is the meaning of the play. I have to confess that what seems to me obvious, is that the promised supersession of justice by love and mercy does not come about, and that the end is something of a parody of heavenly harmony and love. The play *is* about the qualities he mentions, but it treats them much more critically than he suggests. He seems to have overlooked the irony that is at the centre of its meaning.

To emphasise the importance and centrality of the irony, I would suggest that the play is "about" the manner in which the Christians succeed in the world by not practising their ideals of love and mercy; that it is about their exploitation of an assumed unworldliness to gain the worldly advantage over Shylock; and that, finally, it is about the essential likeness of Shylock and his judges, whose triumph is even more a matter of mercenary justice than his would have been. In this view the play does not celebrate the Christian virtues so much as expose their absence.

Yet this account too, though no less true than the more usual one, would be less than adequate to the experience. For the special quality of the play is that it refuses to endorse any such simple judgements. It compels an intensely sympathetic insight into Shylock's tragically corrupt nature, yet we are unlikely to identify ourselves with him. It reveals in the Christians a complacent inhumanity, and yet we are likely to find them attractive in their fashion. No account of the play which offers to see it in terms of simple good and evil can hope to satisfy. It is too subtle and exploratory for that; and also, perhaps, too ironic in its resolution.

A *"Prima Facie"* Reading

The characterising quality of the Venice-Belmont set is their worldliness. This makes it odd that their claims to represent the Christian virtues should be accepted at face value. With the exception of a few set pieces on the themes of mercy, love and harmony—and of Antonio's partial representation of these qualities—their minds are never raised above the gaieties and good things of the world.

Their way of life and the things which possess their imaginations are suggested in the opening exchange:

[1] *Early Shakespeare* (Stratford upon Avon Studies: 3, Arnold, 1961), p. 224.

Solanio. Believe me, sir, had I such venture forth,
   The better part of my affections would
   Be with my hopes abroad. I should be still
   Plucking the grass to know where sits the wind,
   Piring in maps for ports and piers and roads:
   And every object that might make me fear
   Misfortune to my ventures, out of doubt,
   Would make me sad.
Salerio. My wind, cooling my broth,
   Would blow me to an ague when I thought
   What harm a wind too great might do at sea.
   I should not see the sandy hour-glass run
   But I should think of shallows and of flats,
   And see my wealthy Andrew docked in sand,
   Vailing her high-top lower than her ribs
   To kiss her burial. . . . Should I go to church
   And see the holy edifice of stone,
   And not bethink me straight of dangerous rocks,
   Which touching but my gentle vessel's side,
   Would scatter all her spices on the stream,
   Enrobe the roaring waters with my silks,
   And, in a word, but even now worth this,
   And now worth nothing?   (I.i.15–36)

In image and idiom that splendidly evokes the merchant's compulsive fears and hopes, and his world of profit and risk. The language of the play as a whole is drawn quite consistently from that world, so that the action is firmly placed in a context of worldly preoccupations and values. Venice and Belmont emerge as gay, splendid and rich, and not very near to heaven; their end is profit and pleasure, not perfection.

One set of words recurs constantly in their speech—*venture* and *fortune,* or *hazard, chance,* etc. From the recurrence comes a cumulatively powerful sense that the goal of their endeavours is the winning, metaphorically and literally, of the "golden fleece," a common image for the great fortunes the Elizabethan merchant-adventurers hoped for. But to be committed to the pursuit of worldly fortune is to be subjected, in the medieval view of things, to the whims of the fickle goddess Fortune; at the most serious level, it is to forfeit the redemptive influence of Providence for the chances and reverses of Fortune's wheel. Boethius' salutation to the true followers of Christ in the world, "O happy race of mortals if your hearts are ruled as is the universe by divine love," can scarcely be applied to the Christians of Venice and Belmont. The fount of their happiness is Portia, appropriately referred to as a golden fleece of fortunate beauty and wealth. In consequence their allusions to the values of a world transcending their own, such as divine mercy or heavenly harmony, stand out as precisely that, allusions to quite another world.

But more than this, their worldliness is shown to be of a kind which subverts their religion. In the passage from Salerio quoted before, what we have is not a simple preoccupation with the world, but the expression of that preoccupation in an idiom adapted from the pulpit. It was commonplace to draw from the hour-glass the moral that man's life is brief and eternity his proper end. But Salerio reverses the preacher's logic and draws a wholly secular moral, ignoring any life beyond death. Again, his culminating image, "Enrobe the roaring waters with my silks," very strikingly fuses the splendour and the loss, but without at all heeding the implicit biblical admonition against the vanity of rich apparel. The whole passage is, in effect, a parody of orthodox warnings against putting one's hopes upon worldly fortune, since it echoes them only to reduce them to an occasion for a more anxious concern with the world.

The major instance of this irony is the contrast between Portia as we see her at Belmont, lightly disregarding the bonds of law and duty, and as we see her in the court, disguised as the wise doctor of law. One observation will be enough to suggest how grave the disparity could be, and to what ironic effect. When Portia declares near the end of IV.i, "I was never yet more mercenary," there is a curious and significant effect. The immediate sense, quite innocently playful, is clear enough. And yet "mercenary" is a startling word to have just there, the more so as it echoes "mercy," which would have seemed the obviously appropriate word. Behind the echo, as it happens, lies the fact that both words come from the same Latin root, *merces* (reward or fee). The direct, secular, development was to "mercenary," meaning "actuated by self-interest." But at the same time, through the influence in Christian Latin of the complex of ideas implicit in the Redemption, "mercy" came to mean "pity or compassion" of the sort shown, in its supreme form, in Christ's so loving the world as to die that it might be redeemed from sin. All this is manifestly very relevant to our thinking about Portia, in which a main question must be whether her conduct conforms to the ideal of loving one's neighbour as oneself, or is more nearly self-interested. Coming where it does, with its oddness and ambiguity, that "mercenary" crystallises the suspicion that what we have seen in her is perhaps literally mercenary, and that her appearance as Justice and Mercy has been a most deceiving disguise. There is then a possibility that Portia has outdone even the Venetians in subverting religion to her own worldly will, reducing its supreme principle of generous love to something nearly its opposite. *Can* Portia be said to love Shylock as herself, or as she loves her Christian friends?

However, this ironic questioning of Portia, though it is pervasive, is unlikely to lead us to reject her. What it should do is prevent the uncritical acceptance of her at face-value. After all, one of the main themes of the play is that "the world is still deceived with ornament," and the action is constantly exploring the ways in which the appearance and the reality may differ. The warning to be not beguiled by "the seeming truth which cunning times put on/To entrap the wisest" is surely as relevant to Portia, in her borrowed robes and with her "gracious voice," as it is to Gratiano in his assumed "civility" (II.ii.174 ff.). Shylock's image of "Christian fools with varnished faces" may be apt in more ways than its context at first suggests.

A word here about the way the allusions to the Christian ideal work in the play may prevent some misapprehensions. It is not easy to gauge the exact force of these allusions, partly because they are so variable a quantity, shifting from a subdued presence in Salerio's opening speech to the explicitness of Portia's invocation to Mercy. But it is possible to be definite on the main point, and that is that the Christian ideal is not deployed as a standard by which the characters are to be judged. The controlling viewpoint is not that of the eye of Heaven, but that of enlightened human feeling.

There is a neat illustration in Lancelot Gobbo's choosing Bassanio's world, at the expense of his duty to Shylock, in terms which evoke a morality-play frame of reference (see II.ii.1-29). In fact we don't judge him as a Christian soul, but simply as a sly rogue with an eye for the main chance. The judgement implied by the allusion to the morality play, that he is damned if he do not repent, is distanced and dissolved in the clowning. All that remains of it is a clearer definition of his motives and conduct as a young man in the world of men. It is the same with the Christians in general. The play does not imply, for example, that they ought to be ideally merciful; nor that they are damned for falling short of the ideal or subverting it. The dramatic experience simply does not lead us to judge them in relation to the ideal; it leads us to judge them by their treatment of Shylock. Their offence is not against God but against humanity. The function of the allusions to the Christian ideal is to sharpen our awareness of the human issue, but not to be a measure of it. Their function may be likened to that of the coloured spectacles that went with the early 3D pictures: when one looks through them the images assume definition and depth. They are there to be looked through, not to be looked at.

The need for a detached and critical approach is brought home still more when we consider Shylock's part. For while he is grievously wronged by the Christians, to the extent that his inhumanity is effectively their doing, he must nevertheless be held fully responsible for the inhuman act he proposes. Yet again, while the judgement the Christians pass on him is fully deserved, we cannot but feel that his human-ity is larger in scope and depth than theirs. In consequence his defeat at their hands seems to involve a reversal of the right order of things, the lesser being allowed to put down the greater.

John Russell Brown has shown that in the theatre it has always been Shylock's play,[2] and there is good reason for this. Where the Christians speak with quibbling wit or rhetoric, filtering emotion through artifice, Shylock's speech is directly responsive to his burden of personal and racial experience, with the result that his humanity is so much more fully present to us. To take just one instance. In III.i he answers Salerio's "thou wilt not take his flesh—what's that good for?" with this terrible directness: "To bait fish withal! If it will feed nothing else, it will feed my revenge." This reveals far more than the mere desire for revenge. There is an element of wild desperation, indicating the root of that desire in some deep outrage or frustration; and there is a de-spairing sense of the futility of the revenge, since the pound of flesh cannot heal the real hurt. Through the intense realism of his image we can feel the fermenting pressures which have made him what he is. He is no simple devil or machiavel, but a man who sees and feels and thinks as other men do, except that his feeling and thinking has been terribly twisted by the wrong done to him. As Traversi wrote, Shylock "is one of the first of Shakespeare's characters to require of us, like so many of the later tragic heroes, a response in which different and even contradictory judgements are simultaneously evoked." [3]

All this must complicate and deepen the interest of the play beyond any simple issue of the good *v.* the damned. The play confronts us rather with the triumph of a group of worldly and a-moral characters over one whose evil is inseparable from his larger humanity. There is much that is baffling in this spectacle of the breaking by a set of trifling gilded youth of a man with something of the stature and interest of a tragic figure. But we must not attempt to evade or to oversimplify the experience. It is only by making sense of what baffles us that we can attain a full understanding of the play.

* * *

We are subjected disturbingly to two different and unresolved sorts of justice, two different and unresolved standards of value. This is the main challenge for the producer, or for the reader producing the play in his own imagination: how to preserve the disturbing differences of mode and feeling, and nevertheless to resolve them into a coherent meaning. If they are not preserved the play will be oversimplified; if

[2] "The Realisation of Shylock: a theatrical criticism," in *Early Shakespeare* (Strat-ford upon Avon Studies: 3).

[3] *The Pelican Guide to English Literature: 2*, p. 185 (q.v.).

they are not resolved it will seem an enigma, or simply unsuccessful. It seems to me that the differences are resolved by the operation of a powerful and pervasive irony, an irony which carries into the comedy a seriously critical awareness of what has been felt and understood in the tragic part, and which, while it does not destroy the comedy, causes us to judge it by values which it fails to comprehend.

For the irony to be effective it is necessary that the tragic and the comic elements be kept distinct and separate—one remarks how naturally they separate out with Shylock's departure. This separateness is, in the first place, a safeguard against melodrama. If the two elements were resolved into a single mode it would almost inevitably support the black *v.* white action described by Shackford.[4] Beyond this, the separateness is positively the condition upon which the two elements are brought into an actively ironic relation. It is precisely by virtue of the clear disparity and opposition, the contradiction of the more profound by the superficial moral sense, that we are roused to seek an appropriate resolution, a unifying vision.

We can get further towards defining the interaction of the two parts by considering the effect of each separately, and then seeing the separate effects in relation to each other. The appeal of the comic part, with its wit, spectacle and diverting plot, is to the eye and ear, to the head rather than the heart. But the tragic part does "speak to the heart," and engages before anything else our feelings of terror and pity. Our attitudes to Shylock are directly controlled by a quite full emotional response. With Venice and Belmont we must reflect upon the entertaining spectacle in order to discover how we might feel about it; they require our critical attention, but leave our feelings relatively disengaged.

In this difference we have a clue to the dramatic relation of the two parts. Given the Christians alone we could doubtless think our way to a justly judging response. But given Shylock as well we are much more powerfully and directly impelled towards that response. The feelings generated by Shylock must radically influence our sense of the Christians, sharpening and clarifying our attitude to them.

Our feelings instruct us that Shylock is inhuman because inhumanly abused. At the same time we are offered the spectacle of those who abuse him disporting themselves without any trace of guilt. But the play directs us towards a resolution of the disparity by the stronger dramatic force of the tragic part. We discover, I think, that the heart is instructing the head in the right understanding of the comedy, bringing the mind to perceive in the self-centredness and self-satisfaction of the Christians the true cause of Shylock's condition. In conse-

[4] "The Bond of Kindness: Shylock's Humanity," *University of Kansas City Review,* Winter 1954, pp. 85–91.

quence what they offer for our diversion ceases to please, for the heart
is sensible of its connection with evil. The comedy can only exacerbate
this sense, most especially in the last act which follows so closely upon
the trial, with the result that it ceases to be simply comic, and becomes
transformed by a profound irony.

The resolution effected by this irony is primarily a matter of en-
abling us to see the bafflingly doublefaced Christians in a single focus,
to hold together in the mind's eye their attractive appearance and the
vanities and inhumanity which have been exposed beneath it. But
the irony then extends beyond the characters, to involve and question
the attitudes of the audience, in somewhat the manner suggested by
Shackford. So far as we have been attracted to the happily amoral
Christians, accepted them at face value, and rejoiced in their good
fortune, we may find ourselves exposed, like them, to the criticism of
Shylock's fate and of the lesser evocation of a finer harmony.

The tone of the ending has much of the ironic reserve of Christ's
praise of the bad steward, "for the children of this world are in their
generation wiser than the children of light." For the several sins of
commission and omission which we have witnessed, while they do not
disturb Belmont's light happiness, do firmly delimit it, and place it in
relation to the grand framework of heaven and hell. We are made
aware—though the knowledge is lightly borne—that this happiness
depends upon the breaking of Shylock, and the forgetting that he has
been broken; and that it depends also upon the breaking of the spirit
of divine and natural law, and the forgetting about the spirit under
colour of conforming to the letter. If we are invited therefore to recog-
nise and endorse an image of the way we ordinarily live and judge,
by the "decent average," we are shown at the same time the meaning
of our complacency. If this is our paradise, it is the paradise of fools.

Yet the most teasing and disturbing quality of the play is that we
are shown at the same time the meaning of our complacency. If this is
our paradise, it is the paradise of fools.

Yet the most teasing and disturbing quality of the play is that we are
left to rejoice there if we will. The unpurged abyss of guilt represented
by Shylock, and the unattained heaven of harmonious love, however
critical their bearing upon it, may be lightly set aside in Belmont in
favour of the moonshine. Yet what is enjoyed in Belmont is attuned
to our dreams rather than our necessities, and satisfies no more than
our illusions. If we are grateful that the play treats these so kindly,
yet the gratification must be slight and shallow. And we can hardly
avoid having it soured by the consciousness that it is so. For while the
conclusion offers to flatter our fantasies as magazine fiction does, it
embodies also, as such fictions rarely do, an ironic comprehension of
reality. How many, aware of all that has passed in the play, will rest

content with Belmont? and how many will be uncritically content with the standard of average decency in the face of what it could do to Shylock? Our ordinary worldly standards must come to seem less than adequate to the more serious occasions of life touched upon by the play.

Not that the play will purge us of our inadequacies in the matter, or of the follies of the world. Perhaps it would be a more comfortable play if it did in some way or other. Tragedy might purge us of the guilt of being as we are; and comedy reconcile us to ourselves through laughter. But the achievement of this play is in its not fitting cleanly into either mode, and instead confronting us deliberately with an image of our ordinary condition of moral compromise, of complacent spiritual mediocrity. The play neither condemns nor condones that condition: it reflects it accurately, thereby to promote a better knowledge of ourselves. The end makes us aware, even as it invites us to relapse into it, that the cosy amorality in which we would live if we were left to, is not ideal, is not the heaven of perfection we would like to think we aspire to.

We are tempted to look to literature to flatter our illusions of moral grandeur, to show us ourselves in the parts of saint or sinner, hero or martyr. But *The Merchant of Venice* offers to reflect what we are in our ordinary varnished reality. If we find this intolerable it is perhaps because we feel naked without our illusions. The emperor was proud until told he was without clothes.

Nevill Coghill: The Theme of *The Merchant of Venice*

A director of *The Merchant of Venice* is faced by a seeming problem. It clearly has to do with an enmity between a Jew and a Christian. Is then its theme the racial and religious conflict of character? Should a producer take sides? if so, can he please himself as to which side he takes? The title page of the second quarto reads:

> The Excellent History of The Merchant of Venice. With the extreme cruelty of Shylocke the Iew towards the saide Merchant, in cutting a iust pound of his flesh. . . .

This announcement seems to justify an anti-Semitic slant; yet, if a producer attempts one, he finds himself presently faced with moments of dialogue utterly intractable to such interpretation:

"*The Theme of* The Merchant of Venice (*Editor's title*). From Shakespeare Criticism 1935–60, by Nevill Coghill, ed. Anne Ridler (London: Oxford University Press, 1963), pp. 213–20. Reprinted by permission of the author.

> *Shylock.* Shall I bend low, and in a bond-mans key
> With bated breath, and whispring humblenesse,
> Say this: Faire sir, you spet on me on Wednesday last;
> You spurn'd me such a day; another time
> You cald me dog; and for these curtesies
> Ile lend you thus much moneyes.
> *Ant.* I am as like to call thee so againe,
> To spet on thee againe, to spurne thee too.

Or

> Hath not a *Iew* eyes? hath not a *Iew* hands, organs, dementions, senses, affections, passions, fed with the same foode, hurt with the same weapons, subiect to the same diseases, healed by the same meanes, warmed and cooled by the same Winter and Sommer as a Christian is: if you pricke vs doe we not bleede? If you tickle vs, doe we not laugh? if you poison vs doe we not die?

The great speech from which these lines come—and there are others like it—make it impossible to carry through an anti-Semitic presentation of the play; on the other hand, to regard Shylock as the wronged hero of an oppressed race falling with final grandeur to a verbal quibble, cannot be reconciled with the last Act, in which the agents of his fall gather by moonlight for their joys in Belmont. Is he to perish and are they to be rewarded?

If then the play will work neither as a Jew-baiter, nor as its opposite, there is nothing to conclude except that either Shakespeare did not know his business, or we have misunderstood it. The latter is the more likely: the title page of Quarto may have misled us. We must try again, and seek a unifying theme that will include these opposites of race and religion.

There is such a theme and it has a long tradition; its best expression is in *Piers Plowman*. It is the theme of Mercy against Justice. In that poem, Truth, who is God, sent Piers a Pardon for the world. All in two lines it lay:

> Et qui bona egerunt ibunt in vitam eternam
> Qui vero mala in ignem eternum.

"Those who do well shall go into eternal life: but those indeed who do evil, into eternal fire." In what sense this is a pardon is hard to see, for it states an exactly proportionate requital, an eye for an eye, a tooth for a tooth, as the principle of reward and punishment; this may be justice but where is the pardon? Where is Mercy?

The poem leaves us unsatisfied of an immediate answer, but opens a labyrinth of inquiry that leads to the story of the Incarnation, the

Passion, the Crucifixion, and Descent into Hell. And in Hell, in a great speech, Christ argues His own payment of man's debt:

> *Ergo,* soule shal soule quyte . & synne to synne wende,
> And al þat man hath mysdo . I, man, wyl amende.[1]

His payment on Calvary is available to all who acknowledge their debt, says the poet, and render their dues in confession and obedience; for to do this is to do well, and therefore to go into eternal life.

Now Christ's right to enter Hell and despoil the Fiend of his prey in this manner is formally debated in the poem by the Four Daughters of God, Mercy and Truth, Righteousness and Peace. Briefly their argument is this: under the Old Law, God ordained punishment for sin in Hell, eye for eye and tooth for tooth. But under the New Law of His ransom paid on Calvary, He may with perfect justice redeem "those that he loved," and this justice is His mercy. The New Law does not contradict, but complements the Old. Mercy and Truth are met together, Righteousness and Peace have kissed each other.

Almost exactly the same argument is conducted by the same four daughters of God at the end of *The Castle of Perseverance,* a morality play of the early fifteenth century. The protagonist, *Humanum Genus,* dies in sin and comes up for judgment. Righteousness and Truth demand his damnation, which the play would show to be just. Mercy and Peace plead the Incarnation, and *Humanum Genus* is saved.

Now if we allow this Christian tradition of a former age to show us a pathway into Shakespeare, it will lead us to a theme that can make a unity of *The Merchant of Venice,* and solve our dilemma.

The play can be seen as a presentation of the theme of Justice and Mercy, of the Old Law and the New. This puts an entirely different complexion upon the conflict of Jew and Gentile. The two principles for which, in Shakespeare's play, respectively, they stand, are both inherently right. They are only in conflict because, whereas God is held to be absolutely just as He is absolutely merciful, mortal and finite man can only be relatively so, and must arrive at a compromise. In human affairs either justice must yield a little to mercy, or mercy to justice; the former solution is the triumph of the New Law, and the conflict between Shylock and Portia is an *exemplum* of this triumph. I do not wish to suggest that Portia or Shylock are allegorical figures in the sense that *Wikked-Tunge* or *Bialacoil* are in the *Romaunt of the Rose,* for these are only abstractions; but they are allegorical in the sense that they adumbrate, embody, maintain, or stand for these concepts, while remaining individuals in fullest humanity. Shylock, there-

---

[1] Therefore soul shall pay for soul and sin shall return to sin
And all that man has misdone, I, man, will amend.
                                   Piers Plowman B xviii.338-9.

fore, should seem a great Old Testament figure, a patriarch perhaps, standing for the Law; and he will be tricked, just as Satan was tricked by the Incarnation, according to the tradition of the Middle Ages. A *Bestiary* of the thirteenth century tells us that no Devil-hunter knew the secret way by which Christ the Lion came down and took His den on earth:

> Migte neure diuel witen,
> þog he be derne hunte,
> hu he dun come,
> Ne wu he dennede him
> in þat defte meiden,
> Marie bi name . . .[2]

And *Piers Plowman* has a like idea:

> . . . the olde lawe graunteth
> That gylours be bigiled . and that is gode resoun
> *Dentem pro dente, & oculum pro oculo.*[3]

We must not, therefore, think the ruse by which Portia entraps Shylock is some sly part of her character, for it is in the tradition; besides she gives Shylock every chance. Thrice his money is offered him. He is begged to supply a surgeon. But no, it is not in the bond. From the point of view of the medium of theater, the scene is, of course, constructed on the principle of peripeteia, or sudden reversal of situation, one of the great devices of dramaturgy. At one moment we see Mercy a suppliant to Justice, and at the next, in a flash, Justice is a suppliant to Mercy. The reversal is as instantaneous as it is unexpected to an audience that does not know the story in advance. Portia plants the point firmly:

> Downe, therfore, and beg mercy of the Duke.

And, in a twinkling, mercy shows her quality:

> *Duke.* That thou shalt see the difference of our spirit,
> I pardon thee thy life before thou aske it;
> For halfe thy wealth, it is *Anthonio's,*
> The other halfe comes to the generall state,
> Which humblenesse may driue vnto a fine.

Out of this there comes the second reversal. Shylock, till then pursuing Antonio's life, now has to turn to him for favor; and this is Antonio's response:

[2] No fiend was able to know, cunning hunter though he be, how he came down, or how he took his den in that deft Maiden, Mary by name.
[3] The Old Law allows that those who use trickery should be tricked themselves; and that is good reasoning. A tooth for a tooth and an eye for an eye.

> So please my Lord the Duke, and all the Court
> To quit the fine for one halfe of his goods,
> I am content; so he will let me haue
> The other halfe in vse, to render it
> Vpon his death, vnto the Gentleman
> That lately stole his daughter.
> Two things prouided more, that for this fauour
> He presently become a Christian:
> The other, that he doe record a gift
> Heere in the Court of all he dies possest
> Vnto his sonne *Lorenzo,* and his daughter.

Evidently Antonio recognizes the validity of legal deeds as much as
Shylock does, and his opinion on Jessica's relationship with Lorenzo
is in agreement with Shakespeare's, namely that the bond between
husband and wife overrides the bond between father and daughter.
Cordelia and Desdemona would have assented. Nor is it wholly alien
to Shylock who is himself a family man. For him to provide for Jessica
and Lorenzo is not unnaturally harsh.

It is Antonio's second condition that seems to modern ears so fiercely
vindictive. In these days all good humanitarians incline to the view
that a man's religion is his own affair, that a religion imposed is a
tyranny, and that one religion is as good as another, if sincerely followed.

But the Elizabethans were not humanitarians in this sense. Only in
Utopia, where it was one of "the auncientest lawes among them that
no man shall be blamed for reasonynge in the mayntenaunce of his
owne religion" (and Utopia was not in Christendom) would such views
have seemed acceptable. Whether we dislike it or not, Shylock had no
hope, by Elizabethan standards, of entering a Christian eternity of
blessedness; he had not been baptized. It would not have been his
cruelty that would have excluded him (for cruelty, like other sin,
can be repented) but the simple fact that he had no wedding garment.
No man cometh to the Father but by me.

Shylock had spent the play pursuing the mortal life of Antonio
(albeit for private motives) in the name of justice. Now, at this reversal,
in the name of mercy, Antonio offers him the chance of eternal life,
his own best jewel.

It will, of course, be argued that it is painful for Shylock to swallow
his pride, abjure his racial faith, and receive baptism. But then Christianity is painful. If we allow our thoughts to pursue Shylock after he
left the Court we may well wonder whether his compulsory submission
to baptism in the end induced him to take up his cross and follow
Christ. But from Antonio's point of view, Shylock has at least been

given his chance of eternal joy, and it is he, Antonio, that has given it to him. Mercy has triumphed over justice, even if the way of mercy is a hard way.

Once this aspect of the Trial scene is perceived, the Fifth Act becomes an intelligible extension of the allegory (in the sense defined), for we return to Belmont to find Lorenzo and Jessica in each other's arms. Christian and Jew, New Law and Old, are visibly united in love. And their talk is of music, Shakespeare's recurrent symbol of harmony.

It is not necessary for a single member of a modern audience to grasp this study in justice and mercy by any conscious process during a performance, or even afterwards in meditation. *Seeing one may see and not perceive.* But a producer who wishes to avoid his private prejudices in favor of Shakespeare's meanings, in order that he may achieve the real unity that binds a poetical play, should try to see them and to imagine the technical expedients of production by which that unity will be experienced. If he bases his conception on the resolution of the principles of justice and mercy, he will then, on the natural plane, be left the freer to show Christians and Jews as men and women, equally endowed with such faults and virtues as human beings commonly have.

W. H. Auden: Belmont and Venice

Shylock is a miser and Antonio is openhanded with his money; nevertheless, as a merchant, Antonio is equally a member of an acquisitive society. He is trading with Tripoli, the Indies, Mexico, England, and when Salanio imagines himself in Antonio's place, he descrbes a possible shipwreck thus:

> . . . the rocks
> Scatter all her spices on the stream,
> Enrobe the roaring waters with my silks.

The commodities, that is to say, in which the Venetian merchant deals are not necessities but luxury goods, the consumption of which is governed not by physical need but by psychological values like social prestige, so that there can be no question of a Just Price. Then, as regards his own expenditure, Antonio is, like Shylock, a sober merchant who practices economic abstinence. Both of them avoid the carnal music of this world. Shylock's attitude towards the Masquers

"Belmont and Venice" (Editor's title). From The Dyer's Hand and Other Essays by W. H. Auden (New York: Random House, Inc., 1962), pp. 232-35. Copyright © 1962 by W. H. Auden. Reprinted by permission of Random House, Inc., and Faber and Faber, Ltd.

> Lock up my doors and when you hear the drum
> And the vile squeaking of the wry-necked fife
> Clamber not you up the casement then,
> Let not the sound of shallow foppery enter
> My sober house

finds an echo in Antonio's words as a scene later:

> Fie, fie, Gratiano. Where are all the rest?
> Tis nine o'clock: our friends all stay for you.
> No masque to-night—the wind is come about.

Neither of them is capable of enjoying the carefree happiness for which Belmont stands. In a production of the play, a stage director is faced with the awkward problem of what to do with Antonio in the last act. Shylock, the villain, has been vanquished and will trouble Arcadia no more, but, now that Bassanio is getting married, Antonio, the real hero of the play, has no further dramatic function. According to the Arden edition, when Alan McKinnon produced the play at the Garrick theatre in 1905, he had Antonio and Bassanio hold the stage at the final curtain, but I cannot picture Portia, who is certainly no Victorian doormat of a wife, allowing her bridegroom to let her enter the house by herself. If Antonio is not to fade away into a nonentity, then the married couples must enter the lighted house and leave Antonio standing alone on the darkened stage, outside the Eden from which, not by the choice of others, but by his own nature, he is excluded.

Without the Venice scenes, Belmont would be an Arcadia without any relation to actual times and places, and where, therefore, money and sexual love have no reality of their own, but are symbolic signs for a community in a state of grace. But Belmont is related to Venice though their existences are not really compatible with each other. This incompatibility is brought out in a fascinating way by the difference between Belmont time and Venice time. Though we are not told exactly how long the period is before Shylock's loan must be repaid, we know that it is more than a month. Yet Bassanio goes off to Belmont immediately, submits immediately on arrival to the test of the caskets, and has just triumphantly passed it when Antonio's letter arrives to inform him that Shylock is about to take him to court and claim his pound of flesh. Belmont, in fact, is like one of those enchanted palaces where time stands still. But because we are made aware of Venice, the real city, where time is real, Belmont becomes a real society to be judged by the same standards we apply to any other kind of society. Because of Shylock and Antonio, Portia's inherited fortune becomes real money which must have been made in this world, as all fortunes are made, by toil, anxiety, the enduring and inflicting of suffering. Portia we can admire because, having seen her leave her Earthly Paradise to do a good deed in this world (one notices, incidentally, that in this world she appears in disguise), we know that she is aware of her wealth as a moral responsibility, but the other inhabitants of Belmont, Bassanio, Gratiano, Lorenzo and Jessica, for all their beauty and charm, appear as frivolous members of a leisure class, whose carefree life is parasitic upon the labors of others, including usurers. When we learn that Jessica has spent fourscore ducats of her father's money in an evening and bought a monkey with her mother's ring, we cannot take this as a comic punishment for Shylock's sin of avarice; her behavior seems rather an example of the opposite sin of conspicuous waste. Then, with the example in our minds of self-sacrificing love as displayed by Antonio, while we can enjoy the verbal felicity of the love duet between Lorenzo and Jessica, we cannot help noticing that the pairs of lovers they recall, Troilus and Cressida, Aeneas and Dido, Jason and Medea, are none of them examples of self-sacrifice or fidelity. Recalling that the inscription on the leaden casket ran, "Who chooseth me, must give and hazard all he hath," it occurs to us that we have seen two characters do this. Shylock, however unintentionally, did, in fact, hazard all for the sake of destroying the enemy he hated, and Antonio, however unthinkingly he signed the bond, hazarded all to secure the happiness of the friend he loved. Yet it is precisely these two who cannot enter Belmont. Belmont would like to believe that men and women are either good or bad by nature, but Shylock and Antonio remind us that this is an illusion: in the real world, no hatred is totally without justification, no love totally innocent.

Chronology of Important Dates

The dates of plays are approximate, and refer to first performance. The dates of other literary works refer to first publication.

	Shakespeare	*The Age*
1290		Edward I banished Jews from England.
1558		Accession of Elizabeth I.
1564	Shakespeare born; baptized on April 26.	Marlowe born; baptized on February 26.
1570		In effect, interest of 10 per cent was declared legal, but taking interest was held sinful.
1576		James Burbage built The Theatre, the first permanent London playhouse.
1582	Shakespeare married Anne Hathaway.	
1588		Spanish Armada defeated.
1588–92	*The Comedy of Errors;* three *Henry VI* plays.	Marlowe's *The Jew of Malta* and *Doctor Faustus;* Spenser's *Faerie Queene* I–III (1590).
1592–94	*Venus and Adonis; The Rape of Lucrece; Richard III; Titus Andronicus; The Taming of the Shrew; The Two Gentlemen of Verona; Love's Labors Lost.*	Marlowe died (1593). Rodrigo Lopez (physician of Jewish origin) executed as a traitor (1594).
1595–98	*A Midsummer Night's Dream; Richard II; Romeo and Juliet; King John; The Merchant of*	Spenser's *Faerie Queene* IV–VI (1596); Bacon's *Essays* (1597); Jonson's *Every Man in*

	Venice; two *Henry IV* plays; *Much Ado About Nothing.*	*His Humor* (1598).
1599–1602	*As You Like It; Henry V; Julius Caesar; Twelfth Night; The Merry Wives of Windsor;* Shakespeare's company moved (1599) to the Globe Theatre; *Hamlet; All's Well That Ends Well; Troilus and Cressida.*	
1603–6	*Measure for Measure; Othello; King Lear; Macbeth;* Shakespeare's company became the King's Men (1603).	Elizabeth died (1603); James I acceded. Jonson's *Volpone* (1606).
1607–9	*Antony and Cleopatra; Timon of Athens; Coriolanus; Pericles; Cymbeline;* the King's Men acquired a roofed theatre, Blackfriars; *Sonnets* (publ. 1609, probably written in the 90s).	
1610–11	*The Winter's Tale; The Tempest.* Shakespeare retired to Stratford.	King James Version of the Bible (1611).
1612–13	*Henry VIII; The Two Noble Kinsmen.*	
1616	Shakespeare died, April 23.	
1623	Shakespeare's collected plays published (First Folio edition).	
1655		Cromwell readmitted Jews to England.

Notes on the Editor and Contributors

SYLVAN BARNET, Professor of English at Tufts University, is the General Editor of the Signet Classic edition of the complete works of Shakespeare.

W. H. AUDEN, perhaps the greatest living poet writing in English, is also a distinguished translator, librettist, and critic.

C. L. BARBER, Professor at the State University of New York, Buffalo, has written on Marlowe and T. S. Eliot as well as on Shakespeare.

JOHN RUSSELL BROWN, Professor and Head of the Department of Drama and Theatre Arts at the University of Birmingham, is a distinguished editor, critic, and director.

NEVILL COGHILL, Professor at the University of Oxford, has directed numerous productions and has often written on Shakespeare.

HARLEY GRANVILLE-BARKER (1877–1946) had a distinguished career as actor, playwright, director, translator, and lecturer.

FRANK KERMODE, Professor at University College, London, has written widely on English literature.

G. WILSON KNIGHT, Emeritus Professor at Leeds University, has directed many productions of Shakespeare and has written abundantly on Shakespeare and others.

BARBARA K. LEWALSKI teaches at Brown University. She has written on Milton as well as on Shakespeare.

A. D. MOODY teaches English literature at the University of York.

TWENTIETH CENTURY
INTERPRETATIONS

MAYNARD MACK, *Series Editor*
Yale University

NOW AVAILABLE
Collections of Critical Essays
ON

(*continued on next page*)

(continued from previous page)

THE MERCHANT OF VENICE
MUCH ADO ABOUT NOTHING
THE NIGGER OF THE "NARCISSUS"
OEDIPUS REX
THE OLD MAN AND THE SEA
PAMELA
THE PLAYBOY OF THE WESTERN WORLD
THE PORTRAIT OF A LADY
A PORTRAIT OF THE ARTIST AS A YOUNG MAN
THE PRAISE OF FOLLY
PRIDE AND PREJUDICE
THE RAPE OF THE LOCK
THE RIME OF THE ANCIENT MARINER
ROBINSON CRUSOE
ROMEO AND JULIET
SAMSON AGONISTES
THE SCARLET LETTER
SIR GAWAIN AND THE GREEN KNIGHT
SONGS OF INNOCENCE AND OF EXPERIENCE
THE SOUND AND THE FURY
THE TEMPEST
TESS OF THE D'URBERVILLES
TOM JONES
TWELFTH NIGHT
UTOPIA
VANITY FAIR
WALDEN
THE WASTE LAND
WOMEN IN LOVE
WUTHERING HEIGHTS

Selected Bibliography

The books by W. H. Auden and by A. D. Moody, on which the present book draws briefly, are also suggested.

Brown, John Russell, "The Realization of Shylock: A Theatrical Criticism," in *Stratford-upon-Avon Studies 3: Early Shakespeare,* ed. John Russell Brown and Bernard Harris. London: Edward Arnold (Publishers) Ltd., 1961. An approach to the play through a study of actors' interpretations of Shylock.

Bullough, Geoffrey, *Narrative and Dramatic Sources of Shakespeare,* Volume I. New York: Columbia University Press, 1957. Reprints sources and analogues, with a substantial introduction.

Burckhardt, Sigurd, "The Merchant of Venice: The Gentle Bond," *ELH,* XXIX (1962), 239–62, reprinted in Burckhardt's *Shakespearean Meanings.* Princeton: Princeton University Press, 1968. Though sometimes needlessly difficult and ingenious, this is often a perceptive reading.

Evans, Bertrand, *Shakespeare's Comedies.* London: Oxford University Press, 1960. A study of the play in terms of the audience's and the characters' varying degrees of awareness of the true state of things.

Freud, Sigmund, "The Theme of the Three Caskets," *The Standard Edition of the Complete Psychological Works of Sigmund Freud,* trans. James Strachey, et al., Volume XII. London: Hogarth Press, 1958. Readers interested in psychoanalytic approaches to the play should also read Theodore Reik, *The Secret Self,* and Norman N. Holland, *Psychoanalysis and Shakespeare.*

Goddard, Harold C., *The Meaning of Shakespeare.* Chicago: University of Chicago Press, 1951. A passionate attempt to show that Shylock is morally superior to the Venetians.

Stoll, Elmer Edgar, *Shakespeare Studies.* New York: The Macmillan Company, 1927. Drawing on other plays and on medieval and Renaissance ideas, in a long essay Stoll argues that Shylock is comic, not pathetic. Stoll makes a similar point more briefly in his "Shakespeare's Jew," *University of Toronto Quarterly*, VIII (1939), 139–54, reprinted in his *From Shakespeare to Joyce*.

Tillyard, E. M. W., *Shakespeare's Early Comedies*. London: Chatto and Windus, 1965. A readable general appraisal.